CRISIS COMPASS

MICHELE EHRHART

CRISIS COMPASS

How to Communicate
When It Matters Most

Advantage | Books

Published by Advantage Books, Charleston, South Carolina.
An imprint of Advantage Media.

ADVANTAGE is a registered trademark, and the Advantage colophon is a trademark of Advantage Media Group, Inc.

Printed in the United States of America.

10 9 8 7 6 5 4 3 2 1

ISBN: 979-8-89188-162-4 (Hardcover)
ISBN: 979-8-89188-163-1 (eBook)

Library of Congress Control Number: 2025909417

Cover design by Matthew Morse.
Layout design by Ruthie Wood.

This publication is designed to provide accurate and authoritative information in regard to the subject matter covered. It is sold with the understanding that the publisher is not engaged in rendering legal, accounting, or other professional services. If legal advice or other expert assistance is required, the services of a competent professional person should be sought.

Advantage Books is an imprint of Advantage Media Group. Advantage Media helps busy entrepreneurs, CEOs, and leaders write and publish a book to grow their business and become the authority in their field. Advantage authors comprise an exclusive community of industry professionals, idea-makers, and thought leaders. For more information go to **advantagemedia.com.**

06-04-2025 2:52

To Ryan, who taught me that if it isn't bleeding or dying, we can fix it.

CONTENTS

ACKNOWLEDGMENTS

Nancy Wollin, thank you for being my partner through this process. It wouldn't be the same book without your talent.

Heidi Scott, your words inspired me to commit to writing this book. Thank you for sharing your talents with me. Forbes Books is lucky to have you.

To my team at Advantage Media, thank you for keeping the train on the tracks and helping this first-time author navigate an otherwise daunting process.

Patrick Fitzgerald, thank you for recognizing my abilities early in my career. You encouraged me to do things that were hard. You pushed me out of my comfort zone. You made me better.

Mike Ducker, you gave me a seat at the table and showed me the importance of doing something with that opportunity. You taught me to have high expectations because people will rise to meet them.

Todd Taylor, thank you for being my partner for all the years we navigated the complexities of FedEx together. You taught me that lawyers are your best friends during a crisis. And you never—not one single time—let my media statements go out without an edit of some sort. In all seriousness, you made some of the hardest days of my career a little better just by being you.

To my teams of incredibly smart and talented communicators, you all taught me so much. I hope you see yourselves in this book.

To Mrs. Love, thanks for teaching me and my son that practice makes permanent. You may have meant math, but it is true for life.

To Mom, you told me I could do anything. I believed you. Thank you for instilling a love of reading and for never being surprised by my accomplishments.

To Ryan, your unwavering belief in me is contagious. Thank you for encouraging me to chase my dreams. And thank you for pushing me to keep notes on the many things that I worked on over the years so I wouldn't forget my worth. You are the reason this book is no longer in my head.

To Brady and Lauren, you are the reason God made me and why I do what I do. Of all the titles I have had in life, Mom is the one I am most proud of and by far my favorite. Parents love their children, but I also like you both so much. You are kind, smart, witty, and vibrant young adults. I want to be just like you when I grow up. The world is yours; go and do great things.

And to my readers, I hope this book helps you in some way. Take what works for you and leave the rest behind.

INTRODUCTION

I didn't choose to have a career in crisis communications. Rather, it's a career that chose me.

Like a lot of people who graduate with a degree in communications, I started out in advertising, which I like to call the shiny, happy side of the marketing–communications–public relations (PR) sphere. I enjoyed the opportunity to work directly with clients, making sure that they were satisfied with our products and that my company was meeting their needs.

It was exhilarating and fun to focus on proactively helping companies reach their goals. I got to tap into my creativity as I participated in the development of strategic ads, upbeat messaging, and event planning designed to attract customers and enhance their experiences. I continued on this career trajectory as I made my way into the corporate world, combining my creative and corporate learnings and finding expertise in branding and PR. I eventually found my way to FedEx, where I gained even more experience in marketing, communications, and global brand management.

Over the next decade, I worked my way through various marketing roles to grow my skill set and earned an MBA. I was intentional in learning new concepts, as well as staying on top of current trends and technology. I rose through the ranks and into management, and I worked on mastering the digital marketing and social media landscapes and becoming well-versed in leveraging new media tools and technologies. It was a time of rapid innovation and exploration in the marketing and communications field. I spent my time leading teams focused on creating videos and storytelling around a remarkable company, its people, and the great work we were doing for our customers and the community.

When I got passed over for a promotion, I asked my vice president and mentor what I could do to bolster my skill set even further. At this point, I was in the communications department, managing a team of content creators. He said I needed more experience in media relations to be considered for the next level of leadership. I had a choice to make: stay in communications or make my way back to a marketing position that didn't require this specific experience. We had several conversations about this topic before an opportunity was presented to me.

My leadership team asked me to consider a lateral move to media relations management, specifically in the area of crisis communications. At first, I was surprised because it had never occurred to me that a company with the size and reputation of FedEx would invest in me to that extent. I was honored, humbled, and scared. Crisis communications was a big responsibility, and I would be learning on the job. Great leaders know when and how to take calculated risks, and my leaders chose me. And I am forever grateful. While I was new to the area of business, the team consisted of tenured experts in the field who were incredibly willing to help me succeed. They needed a leader, and I needed to learn. And boy, did I learn.

I held that job for four months. And it felt like the longest five years of my life.

Let me explain.

When you see an airplane flying overhead, you notice the sleek configuration of the fuselage and the vast and elegant wingspan. You watch the sunlight bouncing off the shiny steel frame as the majestic flying machine makes its way through the clouds scattered across an azure-blue sky. Then, you see the prominent purple tail with the distinct logo, and you know that the world is running because FedEx will absolutely, positively get it there.

I often refer to brand and reputation as two sides of the same coin. Your brand is what you tell people about your company. Your reputation is what they think of you. The same holds true with my airplane analogy. You see the very specific look of a FedEx plane because it has been crafted to show the world its best features. That is how a brand is built. What you can't make out from your vantage point below, or when a plane is on the ground, is the underbelly of that plane. That is where a brand is vulnerable and where reputation is most important.

Moving from creating delightful digital content to conquering crisis management was an incredibly eye-opening experience for me. After ten years of working to tell positive stories and present the brand at its very best, I now saw all of the dangers and vulnerabilities and areas that could—and sometimes suddenly would—go wrong.

In the short time I was in that role, I dealt with the aftermath of an active shooter at a FedEx facility in Kennesaw, Georgia, and a freight truck accident where a driver crossed the median and hit a coach full of first-generation college students head-on, killing several and injuring many more.

I had to hit the ground running in that position, and there was never an opportunity to slow down. It was rapid-fire from day one.

And if we weren't actively putting out fires, we were anticipating the possibilities of the next ones erupting and planning for how we'd extinguish those flames. The sheer volume of incidents and potential crises and the magnitude of the implications each could have on the company, its team members, its customers, and other stakeholders was not for the faint of heart. I worked on vehicle accidents, lost packages of celebrities with large social media followings, lawsuit threats, unionization rumors, diverted airplanes, facility closings, and an employee's death. So, when I say four months felt like five years, that is what I mean.

But here's the crazy thing. In a way that surprised even me, I knew that I had found my calling. Crisis communications was what I was meant to do.

Four months into that job, another opportunity for a promotion presented itself, so I pursued it. And let me add that the position was one for which I would not have been qualified had I not been afforded the experience to manage crisis communications and act as a company spokesperson. Sometimes, the best path forward is a lateral move.

I got the job and was promoted to director of communications at FedEx Freight and eventually moved into the position of vice president of global communications at FedEx Services. I now serve as the chief marketing and communications officer for the University of Memphis. In each of these positions, I have taken on increased responsibility for planning for, managing, and overseeing the crisis communications functions of the organization. Over the years, I have managed more crisis situations than I can count, and I have the experience—some would call them battle scars—to prove it.

Why I Wrote This Book

My grandmother was fond of the expression, "To whom much is given, much is expected." I have taken those words to heart in deciding to write this book. I was fortunate to find my calling as a crisis communicator. And I know that my experiences have given me something unique to offer: the wisdom acquired from thirty-plus years of developing the muscle memory needed to jump in and manage whatever crisis I'm presented with.

This is not just another book about crisis communications. There are plenty of those already on the shelves. Instead, this book is about helping you develop the confidence you'll need to face any crisis that comes your way. It's about how you can obtain the kind of muscle memory required to move quickly in the face of a crisis situation, even if you've never before faced an actual incident of crisis proportions.

My intention in writing this book is to provide more than interesting war stories and revelations of lessons learned, although I have certainly strived to provide plenty of both. My purpose in penning *Crisis Compass* is to provide a resource that I hope serves as a source of strength and comfort to bolster your confidence when you need it. I get it—how can a book be a source of strength and comfort? Strength in that you have a place to find the tools you need to navigate a crisis and comfort in knowing that you are not alone.

You could find much of the information in this book on your own. It is easy to look for a crisis communications plan template with a simple internet search. You could do some research and find many examples of various types of crises and how companies handled them. You could even identify an industry expert and ask them specific questions about their experiences in crisis communications. My hope is this book will make it a bit easier for you to do all of those things ahead of or while you are facing a crisis situation.

Whether you need help preparing for or confronting a crisis in your own company, are interested in pursuing crisis communications as a career, or are looking to expand your PR skills and knowledge, this book fills in the gaps left when you don't have a lot of experience in crisis management. In short, I am writing the book that I wish I'd been given when I found myself managing my first crisis.

What You Can Expect from *Crisis Compass*

Here's what you can expect from the pages of this book.

In **chapter one, Expecting the Unexpected: The Case for Crisis Communications**, I share why it's important to proactively plan for how your company will respond to a crisis. To demonstrate this point, I take you through the most grueling week of my professional life. I show you what a solid crisis communications plan looks like when it's successfully activated and share some of the most important steps you can take to begin building the infrastructure you'll need to support your business interests in a crisis. I also explore why it's important that your communications team interacts often with every functional area of your company so everyone understands how different scenarios can affect every aspect of your business.

Chapter two, Building Your Crisis Communications Plan, introduces the building blocks you'll need as you start creating a crisis communications plan tailored to your business. I explain the three universal truths that apply to every business: To control the message, you must first control the messenger; everything is public (whether you intend for it to be or not); and successful crisis management requires focusing on roles and responsibilities. I then delve into the details of how to select and organize a winning communications team, including what qualities to look for in crisis communicators. These profession-als are a different breed—proactive, sharp, connected, and capable of playing catastrophes out. I also explain why establishing mindful media relationships and readying certain strategies that you can implement when needed are key to a successful rapid crisis response.

In **chapter three, Practice Makes Permanent**, I introduce the most important tenet of successful crisis communications management: *practice.* This chapter offers a practical guide to readying your company for whatever crisis comes your way. I cover how to visualize possible crisis scenarios and provide a step-by-step guide for envisioning, planning, and executing tabletop drills. I also explain the power of a good holding statement and how you can save your company's reputation by having several versions on the shelf and ready to access for future use. I provide several sample holding statements that you can use or adapt to your needs.

Chapter four, Activating Your Crisis Plan, details what you need to do before and during a crisis. I encourage you to learn what the early warning signs are for a potential crisis that could affect your company and how to take action to prepare for or, in some cases, even avoid an impending crisis. I also cover the do-no-harm rule of crisis communications and introduce the Golden Hour, a short window of time when what you do and say can and will make all the difference in how your company weathers a crisis. I offer a few case studies to show you how some companies got it right and how others famously didn't. And I introduce you to the concept of the strategic pause, identifying when and how to use this powerfully effective communications tactic to protect your brand.

In **chapter five, Strategic Silence: Choosing Not to Communicate**, I explain how the conscious decision to remain silent can put you in a more powerful position than you'd be in after stating your case. I then flip this concept around and show how devastating it can be to your brand if you don't speak up when you should. By the end of this chapter, you'll be able to discern whether and when it's time to speak up or keep silent.

Chapter six, Document Everything—Always, introduces documentation as the cornerstone of effective crisis communications. I discuss the importance of documenting everything you and your team see, read, and hear before, during, and after a crisis and provide examples of the types of information you should be gathering and preserving. I also offer a guide to setting up and maintaining your company's documentation infrastructure and then explain what information you should protect and how to determine what you can share and with whom. I discuss the importance of situation reports to keep leadership informed so you and your team can focus on managing the crisis. Finally, I provide templates for converting all that documentation into either a robust postcrisis report or a more limited and precise incident report.

Chapter seven, Seeking Out and Accepting Help, introduces another universal truth of crisis management: You are going to need to ask for help from time to time. In this chapter, I offer suggestions for leveraging your company's internal resources when possible and for seeking help through external resources, such as a crisis management consultant or PR firm, when necessary. I also emphasize the importance of networking in finding outside help that meets your needs and your budget. This chapter also discusses another important aspect of crisis management, which is recognizing that others in your organization and your community want and need to support their colleagues and friends in need. It's up to you, as the crisis communications lead, to help find ways to let them share in healing and rebuilding after a crisis.

In **chapter eight, Leading with Your Head and Your Heart**, I offer leadership advice gleaned from more than twenty years of leading crisis communications teams. I discuss the perils of micromanaging, the importance of recognizing and addressing signs of burnout, and how to make the best use of the leadership shadow you cast over your team. I talk about how fear of missing out (FOMO) is real in our industry and how to address it with your team. And I offer tools for handling the inevitable postcrisis letdown that teams often experience following a particularly challenging situation. To me, this is the most important chapter in the book for leaders. The entire book can be used by anyone managing a crisis situation, but this chapter focuses on being a good leader of people. Leadership is a choice and a responsibility that I do not take lightly.

Chapter nine, Postcrisis Management: Lessons Learned, covers the never-ending continuous improvement that is part and parcel of crisis communications management. I cover the efficacy of postcrisis reviews—how they preserve institutional memory while acting as change agents to inform your team's progress and enhance its abilities—as well as offer practical tips for holding postmortem meetings. The intelligence you receive during a postcrisis review can also be used to avoid a future crisis or mitigate its impact. I encourage all crisis communicators to use what they've learned from a crisis to pay it forward by sharing what they've learned with others who can benefit from their experiences.

In **chapter ten, Creating Your Crisis Management Tool Kit**, I provide a reference tool for implementing much of the practical advice I've offered throughout this book. This is the tool kit that I wish I'd had when I first started out in the crisis communications field and one that I offer to my clients and colleagues who don't yet have their own. I provide a written pathway to help you identify potential crisis scenarios and create your crisis response team. Next, you're guided to establish a media management protocol, an internal communications plan, and a social media strategy for your organization. Finally, steps for postcrisis recovery are provided. And as much as everyone wants to put a crisis behind them and move on quickly, this is simply a step that cannot and should not ever be skipped.

CHAPTER ONE

Expecting the Unexpected: The Case for Crisis Communications

Whether you expect it or not, at some point, your business is going to face an issue, crisis, or scandal that has the potential to damage your brand and reputation. A partner may leave your practice. An employee might embezzle funds. A tornado could destroy your building. It is impossible to completely prevent bad things from happening to good organizations.

I'm not saying that every bad thing will actually come about. With the right amount of risk assessment and crisis mitigation planning, there's a good chance that you'll successfully avoid many of the situations that have the potential to become full-fledged crises. But there will always be matters beyond your control—contingencies that can swiftly and without warning erupt into the kind of issue that can tarnish your reputation, bruise your bottom line, or, at worst, destroy your organization beyond repair.

To prepare for situations outside your control, you need a good crisis communications plan. And while you can strive to anticipate different scenarios and potential turns of events, you can't possibly prepare a perfect plan to address every aspect of every conceivable mishap that could come your way.

But you can come close.

Using knowledge, experience, and foresight, you can proactively plan for how you will respond when an issue or a crisis of any size comes your way.

Plan Meets Execution: Five Grueling Days

My cell phone rang at half past eleven at night, jarring me out of a sound sleep. I slipped out of bed and held the phone to my ear, hoping the ring hadn't awakened my husband. On the other end was my boss's boss.

"There's an active shooter at the Indianapolis Ground facility, and it's happening now. I don't have much information yet, but it's all over social media," she said.

"I'm on it," I replied, and we hung up.

I quietly made my way to my office, closing all of the doors behind me so as not to wake my sleeping family. This was during the height of the COVID-19 pandemic, and the makeshift home office I'd been working in was about to be converted into a crisis communications war room managed via phone calls and Zoom and Microsoft Teams video conferences.

Over a marketing and communications career that had spanned more than three decades, I'd seen my share of urgencies, emergencies, disasters, and catastrophic events. I'd dealt with cyberattacks, scandals, a National Transportation Safety Board crash investigation, unionization efforts, and issues around the delivery of lifesaving vaccines. I'd guided companies through accidents resulting in deaths, weather events, CEO transitions, and fallout from global trade issues. But I'd never experienced anything like the anguish caused by a senseless and deliberate act of gun violence.

That night, as vice president of global communications for FedEx, I was counting on our proactive and extensive crisis communications preparation efforts to help me manage the information gathering and dissemination for the worst event I had yet to encounter in my career. As I switched on the lights in my office, I took a deep breath and got to work.

> Using knowledge, experience, and foresight, you can proactively plan for how you will respond when an issue or a crisis of any size comes your way.

Preparation Meets Its Moment

I sat down at my desk, fired up my laptop, and started scrolling through social media to watch the breaking news as it was unfolding. I made calls to members of my crisis communications team and quickly set up an open Teams call so people could easily join. Over the next several hours, by monitoring the social media posts and what on-the-ground authorities had to say, we were able to piece together what had occurred until we received a briefing from our own security team.

The first order of business was to create a holding statement for the multiple media inquiries we were receiving. The holding statement let everyone know that FedEx was aware of the event and was working with the authorities to find out more information. By the second day, the shooter and victims had been identified, and the police had released the following information to the public.

A nineteen-year-old former FedEx employee had driven up to the Indianapolis, Indiana, FedEx Ground Operations Center on the southwest side near the international airport just as the eleven o'clock shift change was occurring. A hundred or so employees were exiting the secure area, making their way to their lockers. At the same time, the second night shift was just getting to work, stopping at the locker area to stash their belongings prior to starting their shift.

The suspect exited his vehicle, brandishing two weapons that police described as assault rifles (later identified as a Ruger AR-556 and an HM Defense HM15F). In a spree that lasted just two excruciating minutes, the shooter managed to kill eight people, wound several others, and then kill himself. A handful more would be injured in the chaos that ensued during and after the shooting. The victims ranged in age from nineteen to seventy-four.

Over the next week, the FedEx communications team, operating out of the virtual war room, set about doing our job, namely supporting the crisis management team as we worked to ensure our people and the FedEx brand were taken care of.

Addressing Our Stakeholders and Their Needs

In any crisis situation, there are a number of stakeholders in need of protection, attention, and information. In broad terms, our stakeholders were our team members, the victims' families, leadership, our shareholders, and our customers. We also had a duty to be forthcoming with the local government officials managing and overseeing the incident, the community, and members of the press who were reporting about the shooting.

Our first priority, of course, was to take care of our people. The tragedy of what happened affected not only the victims and their immediate families and coworkers but also every member of the FedEx team. Eight of our own had died in a cruel and senseless manner, and many more were injured, both physically and emotionally. From the

CEO to the drivers and package handlers and everyone in between, we were all grieving for our fallen colleagues. We all wanted to find a way to help.

As crisis communicators, our next priority was ensuring the integrity of our brand. There were sure to be questions about how the shooter had gained access to the facility and why FedEx staff members were not allowed to have cell phones with them at the work site. We knew we would have to explain security protocols—including how prohibiting cell phones protected the confidential information of our customers and kept our team members safe by eliminating distractions around heavy machinery—while at the same time taking care not to interfere with the local authorities' investigation. And we wanted to assure our customers that even in light of these circumstances, we were still a reliable business partner.

Falling Back on Drills and Simulations

While I won't say that our war room ran like a well-oiled machine—there are too many moving parts in these types of fluid situations—I can say that we were able to move fast and jump on opportunities quickly. This was partly because we had been in crisis mode since the pandemic first hit in the early months of 2020 and partly because of our foresight in preparing for this type of situation.

Since the first lockdowns, we had all learned how to live in a perpetual state of adaptation. The FedEx communications team had to be in lockstep with operations so we could inform all our internal and external stakeholders about the ever-changing rules of engagement based on the pandemic and how they were affecting operations. We had to be prepared to change our messaging in an instant, and that experience gave us a lot of muscle memory for flexibility and pivoting when necessary.

But I think, even without the pandemic, the FedEx crisis communications team would have been prepared, or as prepared as possible, for these types of situations. We were often sought out for our handling of crisis situations and considered by many to be best in class.

Each quarter, we performed tabletop drills in which the communications team would choose a scenario and then work through the scenario as if it were actually happening. During these sessions, we'd try to anticipate contingencies, think through twists and turns, and isolate the most probable and possible occurrences—and then we'd role-play how to manage each one.

Coincidentally, just a few weeks before the Indianapolis shooting, we conducted a workplace shooter scenario, going through the anticipated challenges and coming up with action plans to address them. Because of this, my team knew exactly what they needed to do, allowing me to focus on overseeing the crisis while looking toward the days ahead and what may be coming next.

I knew that as soon as the team members woke up to this tragic news, they would want to hear from their leadership. So, we drafted a communication from the CEO and made sure it was in the team members' inboxes before they woke up. We also knew that the leadership team would be searching for the latest details of the tragedy that was unfolding on social media and was now on television in real time. I needed to make sure my boss had what she needed to keep key members of the executive team updated. We could not possibly answer every call or provide on-demand updates in response to every inquiry, so we established a set schedule to provide a situation report with the most up-to-date information available at that time to distribute to leadership. We provided these reports three times each day. With internal communications scheduled and channels established, it was time to tackle the business of looking after our people and protecting our brand.

I started with my own team. I needed to make sure that the people who had gotten up with me at half past eleven that night got at least a few hours of sleep. I made sure to bring in other people to cover for them while we all got much-needed rest. It was clear that this was not going to be a one-night event. We proceeded to work in shifts, taking on each challenge as it presented itself while anticipating and planning for each ensuing turn of events.

Our virtual war room operated for five days. Within hours of that initial call, we had issued a holding statement that conveyed the company's sadness and shock at the tragic events and had crafted a message for the CEO to send out to all 550,000 FedEx team members, informing them of what we knew so far about the tragedy. We immediately went dark on social media and pulled any regularly scheduled communications, including press releases and digital ads. FedEx communications were known for being visually cheerful with upbeat messaging, and continuing with our usual designs around the familiar purple and orange logo seemed inappropriate under the current circumstances.

By day two, all social media and other messaging had been converted to gray scale in keeping with the gravity of the situation, and we sent a communications liaison, one of our directors, to coordinate the company's cooperation with officials on the ground in Indianapolis.

We had been in contact with our outside PR firm, which put us in touch with the communications lead of a company that had recently experienced a similar event, and this was helpful in getting us level set regarding what to expect. We now had a presence both at Indianapolis law enforcement and at local government press conferences. We set up a family center in a nearby hotel to provide resources and support for the employees, their families, and the family members of the victims.

By day three, our company representative was participating in local vigils, and we had begun working with an organization to establish a fund for the victims, which we launched with a $1 million donation from FedEx. By the fourth day, remembrance decals in the form of black ribbons embossed with "#FedExStrong" and "Indy" had been designed, ordered, printed, and distributed and were displayed on FedEx vehicles nationwide. And on day five, we formally announced the Indianapolis 4/15 Survivors Fund through the National Compassion Fund and FedEx's donation to all team members, prepared a statement for the upcoming reopening of the Indianapolis facility, and changed the FedEx logo paint scheme of Denny Hamlin's #11 NASCAR car for his upcoming race.

All in all, in less than five days, we reached out to and communicated with each of our stakeholders, showing compassion, support, and cooperation.

Of course, crisis communications must often carry on long after the initial shocks from an incident fade. In the case of the Indianapolis shooting, we continued to supply our regular reports to leadership, kept in close contact with local authorities to offer aid in their investigation, kept the press apprised of new developments as appropriate, and made repeated assurances to our customers regarding business operations. From a longer-term perspective, we made plans to address the milestone anniversaries of the tragedy with remembrance vigils and other tributes to the fallen.

The Anatomy of a Crisis Communications Plan

Most people who are tasked with managing an organization's communications will never deal with an active shooter situation or anything that will grab national and international headlines. But that doesn't mean the crises you and your organization face will be any less significant to your stakeholders or to the health of your business.

The goal of this book is to provide the guidance every business owner and communications professional needs to anticipate, prepare for, and manage crisis communications.

Regardless of the type and size of your organization, the anatomy of a crisis communications plan is the same. First, you will need to build your crisis management team and infrastructure and then identify and practice how to deal with different crisis scenarios. Second, you'll need to understand when and how to implement your crisis plan and practice how and when to act and react under various circumstances. Finally, you'll need to think through ways to deal with the inevitable aftermath of a crisis. By the time you finish this book, my hope is that you will have the tools and the confidence to build a crisis communications system for your organization.

Before jumping into creating an actual crisis communications plan, it's important to understand the critical role communications plays in overall crisis management and why your communications team needs to be fluent in both how your business operates and the ways your customers and other stakeholders could be impacted by critical events.

It's also important to understand why sometimes, when it comes to reputation management during and after an upheaval, the best defense often comes in the form of maintaining a brimming goodwill bank.

The Critical Role of Communications

If you're like most organizations, you already have some semblance of a contingency plan should things go awry. If you live in Hurricane Alley, you know how to secure your offices and protect critical equipment and information systems in the event a severe weather warning is issued. If you are in a professional partnership, you've set up a succession plan and insurance vehicles should any of the partners become incapacitated or pass away suddenly. If you're a manufacturer, you've mapped out what to do from an operations perspective if one of your facilities goes offline or a labor strike disrupts your business.

In all of these scenarios, you've planned out how to keep the proverbial train on the tracks should an anticipated situation occur that interrupts your business operations. That's the foundation of crisis management, and it's certainly an important part of keeping your business going during troubled times.

But without a plan in place to facilitate communications during an incident affecting your operations or reputation, how and when will you inform your clients, customers, investors, employees, and other stakeholders about the situation? Who will manage your messaging and media relations and combat the inevitable rumor mill and social media fallout? How will you ensure your reputation is protected during and after the event?

Making crisis communications preparation a priority—and committing the necessary resources to get a plan up and running before you need it—could be the best business decision you'll ever make. Whether you commit internal resources to developing a crisis management protocol or seek assistance from an outside professional, having a communications plan in place is a vital part of managing your company brand.

In the Indianapolis shooter case, setting up the war room, partnering with legal, making sure that communications flowed to leadership, and managing the narrative were all part of the crisis communications plan. As soon as I hung up the phone on the night of April 15, I knew what I had to do first. Without a plan already in place, given the hour and the shock of the scene unfolding, I doubt any of us would have had the presence of mind to come up with these initial moves on the spot, let alone make it through the rest of that tumultuous week.

THE IMPORTANCE OF UNDERSTANDING BUSINESS OBJECTIVES

Since communications are an integral part of overall crisis management, it's of paramount importance that the individual you're entrusting with your messaging has a deep understanding of how your business works and the underlying business issues impacted by the situation. In the fog of an unfolding crisis, it's easy to get wrapped up in what's happening at the moment and forget how customers, partners, investors, and other stakeholders are going to react to the situation. It's the job of your communications partner to take your business objectives into account when crafting your messaging, even if other matters take priority temporarily.

When I first learned that a FedEx facility had become a crime scene, I immediately knew that a very real and important aspect of managing this crisis would be getting the word out about the extent to which this situation might impact our customers. As soon as we got the green light to discuss operations, our team made sure FedEx was fully prepared to move forward with assurances that we would do everything in our power to keep business flowing. Because our communications team was well-versed in the operations aspects of FedEx's business and had good relationships with colleagues on the logistics side, we were able to accurately communicate how FedEx would handle any temporary closure of the Indianapolis facility in terms our customers could understand. This is a great example of how crisis communications don't operate in a vacuum and should never be siloed away from core operations.

INSULATING YOUR BRAND WITH GOODWILL

Goodwill, the value a company gets from its brand and reputation, is the best cushion you can have in a crisis. The more goodwill you've accumulated, the softer you'll land should your company find itself a victim of circumstances or embroiled in a scandal.

If you're a large company that pours a lot of resources into creating a positive image, you'll be able to capitalize on that brand positioning, especially if your company has a reputation for stellar customer service and engages in highly publicized branding campaigns, such as partnering with charities and supporting popular causes that align with your customer base.

Smaller businesses can build their brands by connecting with the community, earning a reputation for ethical behavior and good customer service, and promoting attributes on social media channels and in marketing campaigns. The more you can show evidence of your positive goodwill—via online reviews and customer testimonials, for example—the better you'll be able to weather a temporary crisis and the more you'll be able to limit the damage.

If you think in terms of banking your goodwill—and consider that you build trust in one-dollar increments but pay for it in hundreds of dollars—it's easy to see that investing in reputation-building endeavors can mean playing a long game, but you'll reap the rewards if and when your business needs it.

ISOLATING THE CRISIS

A crisis for your business is not your crisis. And your crisis isn't your business. One of the challenges of crisis communications management is keeping the crisis from overtaking your organization's overarching purpose. Don't let everything associated with your brand become tainted by an unfortunate occurrence. The most powerful weapon you have to combat false or overreaching narratives is your own control of the story, carefully constructed and thoughtfully distributed through a well-planned and well-executed crisis communications plan.

I like to think of crisis communications as a carefully thought-out proactive practice rather than an isolated reaction to address a particular occurrence at a particular moment in time. If I've done my job correctly, by the time you finish this book, you'll not only have a solid crisis communications plan in place; you will also have the confidence to calmly and deliberately implement the plan the moment you need it.

CHAPTER TWO

Building Your Crisis Communications Plan

There is no such thing as a perfectly planned, ready-to-execute, all-encompassing, flawless crisis communications plan. You will never succeed in creating a finished, polished document that covers all your bases in every potential crisis that could cross your path. A crisis communications plan, by design, must be revisited, revised, and revamped on a regular basis. I refer to it as a living, breathing document.

A static communications plan might suffice if your company remained static or if technological advances and social conventions around how we communicate came to a standstill. But that's not how organizations or the world work.

Businesses grow and priorities change. Products and services undergo improvements. You start off on one trajectory and then find yourself veering off course on another. New attitudes and technology are adopted as the old ways of doing things are discarded. Being in business means constantly evolving and often requires shifting your priorities. And that means you'll find yourself imagining and reimagining the types of crises your organization could encounter and how you'll deal with them.

Similarly, the ways information gets disseminated both inside your organization and to the outside world are varied and in a constant state of change. For internal communications, team email blasts may have given way to more secure outreach via your company's intranet or to direct messaging through a platform such as Microsoft Teams or Slack. Information that you want to share with customers, suppliers, investors, and other external stakeholders has extended beyond direct mail, email, and issuing press releases through wire service distribution channels. They're now social media posts and targeted digital ads leveraging online platforms, such as search engines, websites, and mobile apps.

In the same way that building a business and managing communications are dynamic undertakings, building a crisis communications plan is a constantly changing endeavor that requires continuous upgrading and improvement. In short, a meaningful crisis communications plan is, by design, a perpetual work in progress.

Preliminary Matters: Three Universal Truths

Before you begin selecting your crisis communications team and building your plan, it's important to settle on three universal truths that apply to every organization, regardless of how large, how small, or how many resources you have at your disposal. The first is that to control the message, you have to limit who can act as the messenger. The second is that almost every communication that you and others inside your organization make, even if intended for a limited audience, could end up in the public domain. The third is that an effective crisis communications plan must focus on roles and responsibilities first and individual team members second.

CONTROL THE MESSENGER

Well before any kind of crisis materializes—and, frankly, this is a best communications practice for any organization, whether you're facing a crisis or not—you need to establish internal controls and procedures around who can speak on behalf of the company. Start by designating just one individual to act as the primary company spokesperson and then make sure that everyone in your organization—from the chairman of the board to the person answering the phone at the front desk—understands and adheres to the following:

- Only the company's designated spokesperson will respond to media inquiries or speak on behalf of the company without prior authorization.

- No other individual in the organization may post, share, or comment on social media in a way that implies they're an official spokesperson of the company unless specifically authorized to do so.

- When communicating with anyone outside of the organization—and this includes posting content on social media—refrain from sharing confidential, proprietary, or sensitive company information.

The only way to control your company's messaging is to set up this type of strict policy regarding who is authorized to speak on the company's behalf. Be sure to detail your media and communications policy in your employee handbook, train on it during orientation and onboarding, and reinforce it during staff meetings and one-on-one reviews. *No one speaks to the media or members of the public about the company without the explicit permission of your media relations lead.* Full stop.

Adhering to this policy is particularly important both when a crisis is unfolding and during its aftermath. The last thing you need during a time of upheaval is someone commenting about a situation for which they have limited knowledge, particularly if they are frightened or upset.

PRIVACY IS PRETENSE

Never assume that supposedly private communications will stay confined to your intended audience. Emails can be forwarded. Anything that appears on a screen—a text, a direct message, or a page from your company's intranet—can be photographed and disseminated. Calls and videoconferences can easily be recorded without the participants' knowledge and consent.

Unless you're having a one-on-one conversation over a secure telephone line with someone you trust, assume that everything anyone in your organization writes or says could potentially reach an unintended audience. Understand and anticipate potential repercussions if a recipient of a particular message shares confidential information with outsiders and craft all communications with that reality in mind. I am not trying to be an alarmist, but your job during a crisis is to protect the company's brand and reputation, not to make friends.

ROLE REDUNDANCY RULES

Before I delve into detail about the roles that crisis communications team members need to fulfill in order to be effective before, during, and after the crisis at hand, I want to emphasize an important point to keep in mind as you build your team. Every role in a crisis communications plan, even that of the team leader, needs to have one or two layers of redundancy. And every task and responsibility needs to be reflected in a written playbook that anyone authorized to step in can access.

Your crisis communications management team leader is going to need multiple backups, especially in emergency situations that could last days or weeks. I certainly needed the ability to tap out and put someone else in charge for a few hours during the Indianapolis shooter incident. There's no way I could have kept up with five days of around-the-clock crisis communications management on my own without being able to temporarily hand control over to trusted team members. The same was true for my crisis communications team. Each had a counterpart who could tap in when necessary.

In the fall of 2024, thousands of people and an untold number of businesses in Western North Carolina were displaced by Hurricane Helene, months after the flooding the storm caused. This is a powerful reminder that anytime you have an event that lasts days, weeks, or longer, you're going to need relief players to step in and give your frontline team members a break. This is one of the reasons that crisis management protocols need to be role-centric and reduced to writing, rather than reliant on the presence of particular individuals. As you comb through the next section's discussion about how to build your crisis team, define their roles, and adopt best practices, keep in mind that your plan must stay dynamic and flexible, and the players must be, to some extent, fungible.

Building Your Team

There are certain roles that must be fulfilled if you're going to build an effective crisis communications plan. Regardless of the size of your organization or what kind of resources you have to devote to crisis management, you'll need a designated crisis communications lead, some sort of legal support, and an individual or team to oversee internal and external communications. While there will likely be a good deal of overlap when it comes to who has responsibility for what specific tasks, defining these roles and picking the right team members to fulfill them are the most important aspects of developing a crisis plan that will withstand any situation.

As a side note, if you are in a position to hire a permanent team member for your current staff for the purposes of managing and handling crisis communications, there are some skills and character-istics that I recommend from experience. Someone with a background in PR and media relations is an obvious place to start. But keep in mind that crisis communications are for a different breed. Look for someone who is organized, proactive, sharp, and collaborative, chases the lead (has FOMO), is always on, and is maybe even a catastrophizer.

CRISIS COMMUNICATIONS LEAD

Just as every ship needs a captain, every crisis communications man-agement team needs someone at the helm. This is the individual who will be first in line to get the inevitable all-hands-on-deck phone call and who will be charged with setting your crisis communications plan in motion and overseeing its implementation at every stage.

Unless you're running a huge company with many resources, you're probably not going to hire a dedicated crisis communications professional. Often, the person designated as the crisis communications team leader will already wear one or more hats in your organization. Depending on the size and type of your business, this go-to person could be a member of your marketing and communications staff, a seasoned department manager, or a partner or principal. Your crisis team lead might even be an outside crisis management professional or firm you have prepared to bring on board as circumstances warrant.

The Importance of Empowerment

When it comes to choosing who will lead your crisis communications team, the position the person holds within your organization isn't as important as how effective they will be at managing communications both up and down your company's chain of command. Make sure whomever you choose to oversee your crisis communications is well-versed in your organization's operations, can readily identify your stakeholders, and is intimately familiar with your brand. This person should either be a trusted decision-maker, or they should have access to those who can make immediate decisions.

Most importantly, the crisis communications team leader must be someone that you can count on, no matter what, to be the adult in the room. I don't mean this in a disparaging way—every member of the team will have serious responsibilities, and, if you choose the team wisely, everyone will step up when needed. But the team leader will have the singularly daunting responsibility of being the first to receive the information that a situation is unfolding or has occurred.

This person, no matter what, must keep their wits about them. The crisis communications lead will take charge of activating your call bridge and starting the process of notifying the other team members that it is time to shift into crisis response mode. As the person with the most knowledge and insights into the situation, the communications lead will assign tasks to their fellow team members and be responsible for seeing that the most pressing issues are addressed. As importantly, this person must have the discernment to know when certain matters must be held pending an accurate assessment of circumstances or conditions. As such, this person must be empowered to invoke and implement your organization's crisis management protocols without hesitation or reservation.

> The crisis communications team leader must be someone that you can count on, no matter what, to be the adult in the room.

As the global communications officer and, for this type of major event, crisis communications lead, I was the one who initially received the news that we had an active shooter at our Indianapolis facility. I was the one who opened our virtual war room, summoned the team, and directed the actions of each team member in accordance with preestablished roles and responsibilities. I'll never forget having to prep and then send one of our directors to Indianapolis to deal face-to-face with the families of the fallen and the survivors and witnesses, knowing that he and everyone involved would be forever impacted by the tragedy.

I also had to do my share of saying no to power, withholding information from certain members of executive leadership, as well as staff and the media, until the victims' relatives had been notified and law enforcement investigating the crime gave us clearance to do so.

Despite the emotional toll the situation was taking on all of us, the primary reason we were able to get in front of the events so quickly and accomplish so much in just a few days was that, as the crisis team leader, I knew I had the full faith and trust of the FedEx C-suite. That level of empowerment, more than any other single factor, allowed me to click into crisis management mode without hesitation so my team could hit the ground running and bring our best selves to what was, unquestionably, our worst nightmare.

LEGAL SUPPORT

I am a strong advocate for including a legal representative in your crisis communications management team from the outset. Whether this person acts as in-house counsel or is an outside attorney on retainer, many crisis situations require the guidance of a lawyer both while you're developing your crisis communications plan and during execution. Depending on the type of emergency or crisis you're dealing with, there are sure to be unanticipated legal consequences of your actions when it comes to how and what you communicate to whom, as well as the timing of any communications. The last thing you want is to be blindsided by those consequences after the fact. The best practice is to establish a relationship with an attorney well in advance of a crisis and include them in all stages of your crisis management planning.

When something bad happens—say, your customer information is compromised in a cyberattack, or you need to recall one of the products you manufacture—and your company is either responsible or perceived as responsible for it, you can anticipate that a lawsuit will be coming.

Thinking about how you're going to defend lawsuits is not something you need to be worrying about in the middle of a crisis, which is why you need to be prepared for this type of inevitability well in advance. Consulting with counsel ahead of a crisis will give you insights into things such as what types of matters should or shouldn't be put in writing, when and whether certain phone calls or video conferences should be recorded, and who should be apprised of what during each phase of a developing incident.

Bringing legal counsel into crisis communications planning will not only save you a lot of headaches in the long run, but it could also provide the foundation of support you'll need should you or a team member face a potential conflict of interest. Clarity about what is allowed and what is not from a legal perspective will shield you and your organization from potential threats, both internal and external.

Earlier in my career, I was working as the crisis communications lead for a company whose CEO had become a close friend and mentor. During my tenure at that organization, an employee died suddenly and unexpectedly on the job. With leadership's approval, I had developed a robust crisis communications plan for this company that included the requirement that certain types of issues had to be run through legal before members of the C-suite were brought into the conversation.

On the heels of this employee's death, and while I was engaging in this vetting process with legal, the CEO got wind of the situation and called me. He was not happy. Why did he have to hear about a death at the workplace from someone else? Wasn't I supposed to be his crisis communicator—his eyes and ears for precisely this type of occurrence?

My response was simple and direct. "Sir, with all due respect, you will never get that phone call from me. Per preestablished protocol, I consulted with our legal department first. Everything I know, they know. And if counsel isn't telling you something, there is likely a good reason, and that's a conversation that you need to have with them."

He was still frustrated, but he understood. From my end, it wasn't easy or intuitive to withhold information from someone I held in such high esteem. But these were the communications protocols we had designed well in advance to protect the organization's interests and, frankly, the CEO's personal interests as well. Without those protocols, and in the moment of the crisis, I'm not sure I would have had the presence of mind to think of consulting legal before picking up the phone to inform my leadership about what had occurred. Thankfully, I didn't have to make that kind of on-the-spot decision.

INTERNAL COMMUNICATIONS

One or more individuals in your crisis communications team will be tasked with facilitating communications with your internal stakeholders, including management, staff, directors, investors, and others. Depending on the size and structure of your organization, this function could be fulfilled by one person or broken down into smaller teams to oversee different internal communications channels.

First on your radar will be establishing a smooth communications flow with your organization's leadership. It's understandable that those who are responsible for a company's operations and the safety of its employees will want to know everything as it happens even if they're not going to be on the front lines managing the crisis. You'll want to find a way to keep leadership in the loop without interfering with the integrity of your crisis response. Being pulled away from important tasks to answer calls, texts, and emails compromises your crisis effectiveness.

With the FedEx Indianapolis shooter situation, we met leadership's need for information by issuing three updates a day, every day, at predetermined times. That simple act of setting up a communications cadence reduced the understandable anxiety of company leaders who wanted and needed to stay in the loop. At the same time, this created a predictable schedule for my staff to follow, relieving them of the burden of having to stop what they were doing to answer questions.

In your company, the communications cadence could be as simple as having check-in calls a couple of times a day or, depending on the situation, a quick email summarizing the situation at the end of each day. Regardless of how you communicate and how often, level setting expectations around what will be communicated and when from the outset is a must if you want to operate efficiently and effectively.

Communicating with management is important, but so is letting the team members of your organization know what's going on. You'll need to put someone in charge of informing employees about what is transpiring. That might be someone from your human resources department, or it might be someone from operations—even your COO. Whoever is responsible for communicating with your staff needs to have a seat at the crisis management table and the ability to craft and disseminate important information.

In some types of crises—say, a severe weather event that is interrupting operations or a protest that shuts down part of your school's campus—you will need to have a predetermined mechanism for getting the word out to staff about work conditions and how and whether employees should report in. There might also be instances where you want to be able to check on your people to make sure everyone is safe. Having a designated staff liaison and a predetermined mechanism for back-and-forth communications with employees—be it via company email blasts, text messaging, an app, or a dedicated information hotline—will help prevent chaos, quell rumors, and distribute facts during the situation.

With the FedEx shooter crisis, within the first few hours, we had drafted and distributed a message from our CEO to all employees, informing them of what had occurred and letting them know that we'd be updating them as soon as we had more information. FedEx team members wanted to know how they could help, so we let them know that we would be offering avenues for them to contribute to the healing of those affected, as well as our community at large. Behind the scenes, we were working on developing a fund for the victims' families and a solidarity campaign. Having a preestablished mechanism for internal communications made the tasks of rolling out these programs to a worldwide workforce much easier.

EXTERNAL COMMUNICATIONS

You're also going to need one or more people to oversee your external communications. These brand ambassadors will be charged with protecting your brand and reputation by crafting your organization's messaging. It's their job to act either as the designated spokesperson or create talking points for the individual tasked with speaking on behalf of the company.

Public Relations Manager

Crisis-related PR is PR on steroids. Whomever you choose to lead your PR efforts needs to have the experience and resources to manage your messaging and the media. You'll need to decide whether you prefer to use an agency that specializes in crisis communications management, use existing internal PR resources, or hire someone to oversee that function for your company. Each choice has its pros and cons.

Hiring an outside expert could be your best option, especially if you don't maintain an in-house PR department or don't have a media-savvy staff member with experience in crisis communications. The benefit of going outside your company is you're more likely to find someone who knows the ins and outs of crisis communications. The drawback is that, unless that person or agency has been working with you for a while, they might not know your industry and the operational nuances of your company. You don't want to miss important communications opportunities or fail to recognize the full impact the situation could have on your business going forward. If you do outsource your external crisis communications function, make sure to educate your consultant about your industry and your business.

If you already have a dedicated internal PR team on your staff, you'll want to select one person to oversee crisis communications and act as the liaison between the crisis management team and the rest of the PR and marketing teams. Some companies go with a hybrid approach, bringing in an outside crisis communications and media expert for the specific purpose of managing the PR team during a crisis but integrating that person into the existing team.

Regardless of whether you outsource your external crisis communications, use existing resources, or create some sort of hybrid situation, it's extremely important that the individual managing your external crisis communications is involved in crisis management planning.

PUBLIC RELATIONS PREP

As I mentioned in chapter one, when you're in crisis mode, you're going to need to make withdrawals from your goodwill bank. That means that right now, when things are going smoothly, you should be engaging in regular community outreach, amping up your customer service, and encouraging your loyal fans and customers to write and post five-star reviews.

Encourage your subject-matter experts and firm leaders to write and publish thought leadership articles on LinkedIn and in the business media and relevant trade publications. Well before a situation occurs, you want your clients, customers, and the public at large to have formed a positive impression of your organization and its leadership, one that will keep them loyal to your brand, no matter what type of crisis you face—be it a service interruption, a product recall, a data breach, or some type of issue or scandal.

MINDFUL MEDIA RELATIONS

How your brand will be perceived during and after a crisis is also going to depend, in large part, on how you're portrayed in the media. This is why you need to start creating positive relationships with the media representatives who cover your community and your industry well before a crisis ensues.

Get to know the reporters and influencers that cover your community and your industry so you can establish a collaborative relationship. Invite members of the media to your company and industry-related events, and then make it a point to engage with them. Introduce them to leadership and members of your media team. Offer your expertise as a trusted source on background and industry trends without looking for anything, such as positive publicity, in return. When a reporter contacts you for information or a quote, respond as soon as you can and as thoroughly as you can, always respecting their deadlines.

At the same time, develop a rapport with any social media influencers who have an interest in your field. Like journalists, social media influencers are in constant need of fresh content and interesting stories. Go beyond mere press releases to provide both with breaking news and in-depth interviews when you can.

Making connections and building up your reputation with reporters and influencers take time. Work on building your foundational relationships now so that you can draw on solid relationships when needed. You're going to need that firm foundation of mutual trust and respect when a crisis occurs, especially if you find yourself in the position of having to pivot from proactive goodwill-building to reactive reputation-saving.

Preparing to Go Dark

Sometimes less is more, particularly when you're dealing with a situation that is serious or sensitive. Anytime a crisis involves the loss of life or situations where people have been displaced or are facing other kinds of tragedies, consider going dark on public-facing media and promotions.

This might include pulling back on or even canceling your digital advertising, stopping or toning down your organization's posts and interactions on social media, and canceling or postponing any upcoming public appearances or celebrations. Going dark is a strategy that you'll need to carefully coordinate with the people and departments responsible for handling your advertising, social media, and in-person promotions.

GOING DARK ON DIGITAL ADS

If your company is engaged in digital advertising, it's important to recognize that there's a lot of planning and maneuvering that goes into digital ad production and placement. It's not easy to just go in and pull ads on a whim. Executing a wholesale ad pull in the middle of a carefully planned campaign can be a cumbersome and expensive undertaking. But you also don't want the public to be inundated with upbeat and happy messages that seem tone-deaf to what your company is dealing with in real time.

To avoid a situation where you're scrambling to pull ads in the middle of a crisis, sit down with your advertising team—whether you handle advertising in-house or work with an outside agency—and work out a plan for what to do if you suddenly need to stop your ads from running. Know who to call and make sure the person on the other end of that call understands the urgency and knows exactly how to turn your digital ad campaigns dark.

This preplanning stage is also the time for your digital ad team to think about the resources they'll need should you want a quick turnaround on new digital media responding to the event or situation at issue.

GOING DARK ON SOCIAL MEDIA

Social media posts are another communications vehicle that can quickly become inappropriate or even harmful in the wake of a disaster or catastrophic event. Often, as with paid digital advertising, social media posts are scheduled in advance, either directly on the platforms or via social media planning software. As with digital advertisements, you will want to think about the messages conveyed by any posts you might have in the queue and whether they are still appropriate under the circumstances.

You'll want to make sure your social media coordinator and your crisis communications team have agreed on how the decision to go dark will be relayed and received and how social media posts will be paused.

Addressing Events and Celebrations

It's also incumbent on the crisis communications team to keep abreast of any public-facing events or engagements occurring or scheduled during a time of crisis or upheaval. The best way to plan for this is to make sure the events planning team at your company keeps a calendar that is accessible to the crisis management team.

How events and appearances will be handled will have to be determined on a case-by-case basis. If, for example, your CEO is scheduled to give a keynote or speak on a panel, you can either cancel the engagement or tack on talking points addressing the situation. How to proceed will depend on the nature of the crisis and the weight of the potential repercussions for the company's or individual's reputation.

Depending on the gravity of the situation, consider canceling or postponing large celebrations or galas. Think about what the stakes are if you go forward. There is no one right answer for how to handle a scheduled event during a crisis. The key is to stay informed about what is scheduled, stay in touch with the planners and those involved, and think in advance about what criteria you might employ for determining whether or not to move forward.

In fact, imagining different crisis scenarios and simulating how you and your team will react in various situations are the best ways to prepare for the inevitable crisis that will come your way.

CHAPTER THREE

Practice Makes Permanent

I worked with an executive who once told me, "Never waste a good crisis."

He meant that you should always make the most of what you learn during a crisis. His philosophy was that the more times you experience the turmoil, pressure, and stress of a crisis situation, the better you'll be at handling all types of issues. It's the primary way to create that muscle memory—the one that will help you instinctively know what to do when you're confronted with an unsettling situation. While experience doesn't mean you'll be able to go on autopilot when you face a crisis—every situation is unique, and each time, your reaction will be different—you will get to the point where you feel confident in your ability to navigate complex and fast-moving situations. For me, this looks like seeing in Technicolor, almost as if a switch flips in my brain, and I am able to clearly see what needs to be done in the chaos of the moment. This ability to spontaneously transition into crisis mode gets easier each time you go through it.

Fortunately, you don't have to have decades of crisis management experience to develop great skills. You can simulate scenarios and engage in practice exercises or tabletop drills until you reach a level of permanence that gives you—and every member of your crisis communications team—the competence and confidence to navigate a true crisis.

Practice Makes Permanent

I was introduced to the phrase "practice makes permanent" when my son was in the fourth grade. I watched him go from struggling with math to embracing it as a favorite subject. His teacher, Mrs. Love, changed his mind and attitude about math. She taught him two very important lessons: All of the basics you need to build your math skills are taught in the fourth grade, and practice makes permanent.

Mrs. Love made it very clear that you aren't supposed to strive for perfection, because trying to be perfect implies failure if you make the slightest mistake. She took the stress away and replaced it with the attitude that all you need is the willingness to practice until a new skill is with you permanently. Needless to say, the boys loved Mrs. Love, and so did I. She taught me a valuable lesson too.

Mrs. Love taught me the value of doing a task so often that it comes more easily when you need or want to do it again. The benefits of practicing, I realized, could be applied to crisis communications.

By its very nature, communicating in a crisis is difficult. It is made even harder when the circumstances are unpredictable. So, it is important to be very good at the things you can control and then practice the skills necessary to build confidence for everything else. You achieve permanence when you put in the work.

Football players don't show up for a game without first putting in the necessary practice time. Ballet dancers don't take the stage without having trained through rigorous hours of rehearsal and conditioning. To be the very best at anything you choose to do, you have to put in the work.

Managing a crisis is not an individual sport; it is a team sport. Each player must also practice being tuned into the roles, strengths, and weaknesses of their teammates. A team will only succeed if the players know how to support each other in achieving a common objective. When a basketball team reaches that level of cohesion, they'll be able to adapt their plays to quickly get the ball from one side of the court to another, even if they're facing an opponent with plays they've never seen before. That is how you go from being an NBA team to becoming NBA champions.

It's the same with your crisis communications team. As long as you practice hard, learn each other's moves, and work together toward a common goal, you'll be able to handle any crisis, even if it's one you hadn't specifically planned for or anticipated. That's how you become crisis communications champions.

Full Catastrophic Imagining

The most efficient and useful way to form that level of cohesion among your crisis management team is to spend time imagining and reimagining the types of situations your organization could encounter and how you'd react to each one.

Don't underestimate the usefulness of this exercise. And don't hold back. Let your imagination run wild. When thinking of possible tragedies, catastrophes, or scandals that could shake your company's foundation, go from the probable to the possible to the fantasti-

> As long as you practice hard, learn each other's moves, and work together toward a common goal, you'll be able to handle any crisis, even if it's one you hadn't specifically planned for or anticipated.

cal to the ridiculous. Just when you think you've come up with every conceivable disaster that could possibly enter your world, go back and think of some more. I can't tell you how many times I have worked with teams to create fictitious situations that we thought would never come true only to have something very close to what we imagined actually happen.

Start out with stream-of-consciousness brainstorming:

- An employee is injured or dies on the job.

- Your CEO was spotted at a Diddy after-party.

- A union strike shuts down a key supplier's operations.

- Your factory is in the path of a category-five hurricane.

- Client data has been compromised in a cyberattack.

- Your top-selling product may be defective, and you must issue a product recall.

- An employee mistakenly posts a video from your office Christmas party on your company's Facebook page, showing inebriated executives and employees.

- Your company has been planning layoffs, and this has been leaked to the media well before you are ready to make an announcement.

- Student protesters have taken over your university's administration building.

- A whistleblower claims your company has been violating export control laws.

- An employee is suing your company for wrongful termination and Equal Employment Opportunity Commission violations.

- Your company receives a bomb threat during a controversial public event.

- An employee makes a catastrophic error in transferring funds to a customer, which you must quickly backtrack.

Once you have a list, select the scenario that is most likely to occur. Then, select the worst of the scenarios, no matter how far-fetched it might be. And finally, pick one catastrophic scenario that is not highly probable but still possible. These are candidates for your tabletop drills.

Tabletop Drills

A crisis tabletop drill is a way to map out how your team will respond to a particular crisis scenario. If you're a smaller firm, you might conduct your drills around a conference room table or over Zoom, with participants talking through different scenarios and responses.

Larger organizations might conduct extensive role-playing exercises with assigned team members playing the part of victims or agitators. However you design your drills, it's important to play the scenarios out beyond what may seem like a logical conclusion. Don't be afraid to keep asking what-if questions, challenging your team to adjust their responses as the situation deteriorates.

The following is one example of a tabletop drill scenario you might practice with your team.

SITUATION: A FIRE BREAKS OUT IN YOUR LAW FIRM OFFICE BUILDING

Background: Your law firm owns a six-story office building in the center of a busy city block. Along with your firm, which occupies the top two stories of the building, you have office tenants on the second, third, and fourth floors. The first-floor tenant operates the building's restaurant.

A fire breaks out in the restaurant kitchen, and the smoke alarms go off. Everyone evacuates the building as the fire department slowly makes its way through rush-hour traffic to the building.

Objectives:

1. Test the crisis response team's ability to set up a crisis command center during a site evacuation. How do the team members communicate with one another? How do they identify the extent of the crisis and manage the steps necessary to keep everyone safe? How are they addressing property damage? How are confidential attorney–client and other vital records being preserved?

2. Assess the effectiveness of internal communications channels within the firm and with the building tenants.

3. Evaluate external communications, including media management. Is media on-site? Do you speak to them or provide a statement?

4. Practice engaging with key stakeholders, such as clients, tenants, and employees. What mechanisms are set up to facilitate communications?

Drill Steps:

1. **Initial alert:** How is the fire department notified, and what steps are taken to evacuate everyone in the building to safety? How is client information preserved and secured? How does the team gather information?

2. **Escalate the situation:** The fire has engulfed the building and is now spreading to adjacent properties, which are also being evacuated. TV cameras and reporters are gathering outside. Family members, clients, and others are looking for assurances that their loved ones got out as they see the scene play out in real time on TV and social media. Clients are texting and calling firm employees for information. Rumors are starting to circulate on social media that the fire extinguishers in the restaurant kitchen were not up to code and malfunctioned. People are pointing fingers at the building's owner, which is your law firm.

3. **Decision-making:** Examine who is overseeing messaging. Who is the company spokesperson? Who is in charge of addressing legal considerations? Who is coordinating operational responses, such as setting up employee and client helplines and prioritizing safety issues?

4. **Real-time updates:** Feed additional details (e.g., the fire department has been unable to contain the fire, a tenant is being treated for smoke inhalation, or not all occupants are accounted for) and respond to each.

5. **Debrief:** Conclude with an analysis of the team's performance, identifying strengths and areas for improvement.

Not all drills need to be this catastrophic, complex, or time-consuming. For example, a data breach scenario tabletop drill for a retail store might look like the following.

SITUATION: YOUR RETAIL STORE'S CUSTOMER DATABASE IS BREACHED

Background: You're the sole proprietor of a retail store with both a brick-and-mortar facility and an online store. You discover that your customer database, which contains customer names, addresses, phone numbers, and purchase history (including credit card information), has been compromised.

Objectives:

1. Determine the resources, both internal and external, that you can tap into to help resolve this crisis. Who can you call on to contain the breach, assess the damage, and set priorities for addressing the situation? Who can help you assess legal exposure and the steps required to protect the company and your customers? What is your plan for retaining records? How are confidential attorney–client and other vital records being preserved?

2. Assess the effectiveness and security of internal communications channels with your team, including consultants. Who do you call, and in what order? What method of communication do you use? Phone? Email? Text? Are these secure?

3. Evaluate external communications, including media management. Has media (social or conventional) picked up on the story? Do you speak to them or provide a statement?

4. Practice engaging with key stakeholders, especially customers whose data has been compromised.

Drill Steps:

1. **Initial alert:** How do you find out about the breach and assess the situation? What are your legal requirements as far as notifying those

affected and your mitigation steps? How and when do you notify the customers involved? Do you send them an email? Do you post information on your website? What immediate steps do you take to secure your database?

2. **Escalate the situation:** One of your customers is a social media influencer and has begun posting about the breach. The posts are getting a lot of views and shares. Your customers are starting to call, email, and text you. Your voicemail box is already full.

3. **Decision-making:** Who is reaching out to the influencer and how? Who is crafting your messaging around the breach? Who is in charge of securing the database, implementing remedial measures, and bolstering data security? What are you offering affected customers?

4. **Real-time updates:** Feed additional details (e.g., the influencer's rant about the breach has gone viral, and the mainstream media has picked up the story and contacted you for a quote; your data is being held for ransom; or the data breach is part of a larger ransomware attack) and respond to each.

5. **Debrief:** Conclude with an analysis of your readiness to address the crisis and what resources—such as legal, crisis communications, and technical help—you will need to address a crisis situation.

Or, if you're a manufacturer, a practice drill around a supply chain disruption might look like this next scenario.

SITUATION: YOUR SHIPMENT IS STUCK AT THE PORT BECAUSE OF A DOCK WORKERS STRIKE

Background: You own and operate a midsize manufacturing operation that is dependent on imported tiny metal gears to assemble your final product. The gears are an integral input in the manufacture of widgets, which are used in the creation of a variety of electronic products, including medical devices. Your customers are counting on you to supply them with enough widgets so they can fulfill their customers' purchase orders. The dock workers are striking at the Port of Los Angeles, where two containers of your needed inputs have arrived. Without the dock workers to unload the containers, your inputs are stuck at the port. There is a chance the strike could last weeks or even months.

Objectives:

1. Coordinate with operations, sales, and finance to understand the potential impact of this type of supply chain interruption on the company's financial health and customer retention.

2. Determine how internal communications will be handled in the event of a strike. Who will craft messaging to employees and contractors, and how will that be distributed?

3. Determine how external communications will be handled. What will the timing of communications be to outside stakeholders, such as customers and investors? Who will craft the messages? How will they be distributed? Who will handle media inquiries?

4. Determine who to contact to assess legal exposure and the steps required to protect the company from possible breach-of-contract damages claims or other legal liabilities. How will confidential attorney–client communications be handled?

5. Practice engaging with key customers and suppliers to put a plan in place for a significant supply chain disruption.

Drill Steps:

1. **Initial alert:** Determine how to assess the scope of a supply chain interruption crisis and what elements are within and outside of your control. Coordinate with operations to determine how long you can continue to manufacture with current inputs on hand. When will you run out? Can you obtain inputs from elsewhere to keep your factory going and fulfill current orders? Coordinate with sales to understand how many outstanding purchase orders exist and how they should be prioritized for fulfillment purposes. Determine who should be notified about the interruption and how they will be notified.

2. **Escalate the situation:** One of your customers relies on your products to manufacture medical devices for a company that produces lifesaving diagnostic machinery. The *Wall Street Journal* (WSJ) is doing a feature story on the strike and is covering the effects it is having on this medical device manufacturer, particularly how your inability to manufacture your products is causing a shutdown of its operations because its supplier's orders are not being fulfilled.

3. **Decision-making:** Who decides whether your company will engage with the WSJ? If you decide to move forward, who will act as liaison with the WSJ and other press? Who is crafting your messaging around the strike?

4. **Real-time updates:** Feed additional details (e.g., experts think the strike will last another month, and your customers are canceling orders and going to your competitors on the East Coast; or your employees are taking to social media to complain about your lack of planning and their fears of losing their jobs) and determine how you'll respond.

5. **Debrief:** Conclude with an analysis of your readiness to address the crisis and what resources—such as an outside PR firm or supply chain management experts—you will need to address a similar supply chain crisis situation.

Keep in mind that the challenge in engaging in these drills and simulations—as well as in how you will deal with the actual crisis when it appears—is realizing that you'll never get it exactly right. There will always be factors in play that are unknowable, which is why perfection isn't the goal here. Permanence is.

These tabletop drills are also a good way to anticipate the type of holding statements you want to have prepared and ready to go as soon as a crisis starts to unfold.

Holding Statements

A holding statement is a preliminary communication that is designed to reassure stakeholders that you are on top of a situation, even if you don't yet have anything of substance to say. Proper use of a holding statement can even turn a crisis into a brand-enhancing opportunity.

If you were traveling by air during the December 2023 holidays, there's a good chance you were stuck in an airport, wondering if you'd ever make it to your destination. Like many airlines, JetBlue flights were experiencing significant delays and cancellations, largely because of severe weather and high holiday demand. While stranded passengers—frustrated, fatigued, and fed up with the airline's mishandling of the situation—filled social media with thousands of travel nightmare stories, JetBlue passengers had a much different story.

JetBlue passengers were taking to social media and actually posting praise for the airline's customer service. Same flight delays, same frustrating circumstances, but different reactions.

So, what was the difference?

JetBlue immediately owned what was happening. As soon as the delays became apparent, the airline issued an official holding statement, which it shared personally with customers via email and text. JetBlue also shared the statement on its website, app, and social media pages.

In its statement, JetBlue acknowledged the challenges passengers were experiencing and emphasized their commitment to customer service. The airline apologized for the disruptions, cited the impact of adverse weather conditions across key hubs, and stated they were working diligently to rebook affected passengers and resolve the issue as quickly as possible.

Through this response, JetBlue was providing transparency, empathy, and reassurance while highlighting their ongoing efforts to manage the situation. Further updates were shared through the company's website and social media channels to keep passengers informed about travel conditions and support options.

These initial statements went a long way in helping JetBlue diffuse a difficult situation and maintain, if not enhance, customer goodwill during the crisis. The reassurance and transparency contained in these statements—as well as the extra effort the company took in making sure its reservation kiosks, phone lines, and chats were fully staffed, even if it meant pulling in people from other departments to assist with customer service—turned JetBlue into the unlikely hero of the 2023 Christmas travel season.

As exemplified by the JetBlue case, a well-drafted and intelligently distributed holding statement provides an opportunity to acknowledge that an incident has occurred, express an appropriate level of concern, and assure stakeholders that you are on top of the situation and will be providing updates once more details are available. But a good holding statement is only as good as the actions that follow. This means JetBlue had to be committed to solving the problem with their actions and not just their words, which they did. The goal of the holding statement is to demonstrate transparency and maintain trust while avoiding speculation. In other words, a holding statement is a way to reassure your stakeholders that you are aware of the situation and are actively working on a solution, even if you don't have anything of real substance to say yet.

Holding Statement Database

One of the first things we did following the news of the Indianapolis FedEx shooting was issue a holding statement while the situation was still unfolding. This statement acknowledged the situation and conveyed the company's empathy with the victims and all affected. We also worked overnight to send an internal statement from our CEO to all employees, informing them about what we knew about the incident and assuring them that we would keep them updated.

We were able to move so quickly on these statements because we could pull predrafted holding statements from a database we had been maintaining and adding to for decades. Additionally, during our tabletop drill around an active shooter scenario, we drafted sample media statements from our statement database. Because we had already vetted our messaging through legal and top leadership, we were able to modify the messages around the actual situation at hand and send them out quickly.

I recommend creating a database of generic holding statements that address the top situations or crises you have identified during your tabletop drills. This is one of those situations where built-in redundancy is going to be crucial. Don't leave the statements in the possession of one individual, either as a file on their PC or in printed form. The statements should be maintained in electronic form on a shared drive or environment, such as Google Docs or other document-sharing platforms. If your business is large enough to warrant the expense, there are many technology platforms that can help organize holding statements and even press coverage. But keep in mind that these databases are only as good as the information that is entered, so you will want to ensure that you establish standard operating procedures (SOPs) for how information is entered into the system and that your team is properly trained in these SOPs.

While the statements should not be available to everyone, core crisis communications team members should be able to access the statements. They can then utilize and refine them as needed, adding as much information as possible to convey transparency, genuine empathy for those impacted, and any steps you will be taking to remedy the situation. Anyone with access to your statement database should be informed about your internal approval processes before any company statements are released.

If you find yourself confronting a crisis and haven't yet created a holding statement document or created a database, don't panic. Just look back over the last few years to see what statements your company has released. Use those statements to create a new one that fits the circumstance you're facing.

I'm providing some sample holding statements to get you started. Each should be revised to reflect as much detail about the actual incident as is possible and warranted.

For an incident involving injuries or death:

We are aware of the incident that occurred on [date] at [location]. Our hearts go out to those involved. We are cooperating with authorities as they investigate and will resume regular operations as soon as it is safe to do so.

For a product recall:

Quality is the most important aspect of our business. We are aware that a component of our product has been recalled and are working with the manufacturer to correct the issue. Out of an abundance of caution, we are asking our customers to return their products for a full refund. Our sincere apologies for any inconvenience this may cause. We are committed to making sure that our products continue to meet the high expectations of our customers.

For a cyberattack:

Our company has experienced a cyberattack. We want to assure our customers, employees, and partners that we are fully committed to addressing this situation promptly and effectively.

For a natural disaster:

We are aware of the [natural disaster] that has impacted [location] on [date] and are actively monitoring the situation.

Our priority is ensuring the safety of our employees, customers, and community. We are working closely with local authorities and emergency response teams to assess the impact and determine the necessary next steps.

We urge everyone in the affected areas to follow official guidance from emergency services and take all necessary precautions.

For a pending lawsuit:

We are aware of the legal action filed against [company name]. While we cannot comment on the specifics of ongoing litigation, we remain fully committed to operating in compliance with all applicable laws and regulations.

For an ongoing labor dispute:

We believe that our thriving work environment offers great opportunities for our team members, and we look forward to continuing our conversations to address any lingering concerns.

For a bomb threat:

We are aware of a potential security threat at [location]. Out of an abundance of caution, we are evacuating the area and working closely with law enforcement and emergency responders to assess the situation.

The common thread in all of these statements is letting stakeholders and the public know that you are present, concerned, and committed to being forthcoming. The whole point of issuing a holding statement is to acknowledge the situation so you can then focus on managing the crisis. Later in the book, we will discuss the importance of acknowledging a situation quickly. Silence can be detrimental to your brand in ways that may not be salvageable.

All the effort you put into developing your plan and building your team will be worth it when the day comes that you have to use them.

CHAPTER FOUR

Activating Your Crisis Plan

When I went to bed on the night of April 15, 2021, I had no idea that a mass tragedy was about to unfold at the Indianapolis FedEx facility. I had received no warning about what was going to happen. Even though my team and I had drilled several versions of this type of scenario, finding out that an active shooter situation was unfolding at one of our facilities was shocking.

Most people involved in crisis communications will never encounter such a difficult situation. For most crises that cross your path, you will likely have some indication of trouble before launching into crisis plan activation mode.

Early Warning Signs

Often, impending crises come with early warning signs. Sometimes, the warnings will be overt and obvious, such as predictions of inclement weather that could disrupt operations. Other situations, such as a union strike that could interfere with your supply chain, will undoubtedly have been preceded by signs of labor unrest and attempts at union and management negotiations, all of which would have been reported in industry news. And while nobody may be talking about it openly at your firm, you are probably going to notice if one of your key principals is battling an illness, is nearing retirement age, or might be involved in something that could precipitate a scandal. While you don't have the power to prevent any of these occurrences, you'll see them coming and can get prepared to activate your crisis plan.

I spend a lot of my crisis communications energy paying attention to what's happening with my company and my clients in an effort to stay ahead of any impending issues. When necessary, I ready my team to activate responses if and when necessary. While much of this work, fortunately, will never see the light of day, it is important and necessary to acknowledge what could transpire in order to avoid being unprepared.

In my current position in academia, I am always cognizant of the importance of providing a safe environment for young people to learn and grow. With this in mind, I pay attention to potential situations that could turn into urgent issues to address or even erupt into crises to resolve. There are two situations that have been on my radar quite a bit over the last year.

The first concerns the student protests that disrupted many university campuses across the country in 2024. Rather than wait to see how similar student protests might play out on our campus, my team started working with administrators to ensure existing policies would be implemented around any protests and to handle communicating these policies to students and other stakeholders. Our focus was threefold: protecting free speech rights, encouraging peaceful demonstrations, and outlining the importance of respectful dialogue to ensure a safe campus environment.

Another scenario facing higher education is the enrollment cliff, a predictable decline in college enrollment that is beginning now and will get more pronounced over the next few years.

Nearly 2.3 million fewer babies were born in the United States between 2008 and 2013 than in 2007, a result that some economists link to the Great Recession.[1] As of this writing, kids born between 2008 and 2009 are getting close to graduating from high school, and the lower birth rate means that there will be fewer high school graduates applying for college.

My university is one of 5,819 Title IV institutions,[2] accredited postsecondary schools that meet the Department of Education's rigorous standards for eligibility to receive financial aid, and the competition is fierce for these students. University stakeholders that are paying attention to these developments are busy setting plans in motion to address declining enrollment and the resulting financial fallout expected to materialize as a result. As the school's communications lead, it's my job to help develop the narratives around the university's efforts to attract students to our university. This includes addressing concerns about the value of higher education in general and promoting the value of an education at our school in particular so that students will select us over the multitude of options available to them. In order to achieve sustainable growth, my role is to help navigate the landscape with proactive and strategic communications.

What is going on in your community that could reach crisis proportions for your business? What trends are you spotting, and

---

1   Kenneth M. Johnson, "The Hidden Cost of the Recession: Two Million Fewer Births and Still Counting," University of New Hampshire, Carsey School of Public Policy, Winter 2014, https://scholars.unh.edu/cgi/viewcontent.cgi?article=1230&context=carsey.

2   "The Total Number of Higher Education Institutions Decreases by 2 Percent," National Center for Education Statistics, August 21, 2024, https://nces.ed.gov/whatsnew/press_releases/8_21_2024.asp.

how could they eventually impact your bottom line? As you scan your environment, what situations are ripe to materialize in the foreseeable future and precipitate an activation of your crisis plan?

Of course, all the preparation and prognostication in the world won't keep the unexpected from happening. At some point, you will encounter a scenario that sends shockwaves throughout your organization. In those instances, you'll have to fall back on your experience and your team.

Jumping In, Ready or Not

A few years ago, a beloved kindergarten teacher at my daughter's school went missing. She was an elite runner training for an upcoming marathon. As she was the mother of two young children, early morning runs were the only time she could train. When she failed to return home at the usual time, her husband alerted the authorities. She was presumed kidnapped. Word spread quickly around the school's close-knit community and the neighborhood where the young woman lived and worked. It wasn't long until concerned members of the community began reaching out to the school, looking for ways to help.

A social media frenzy followed as unsubstantiated rumors and inaccurate statements were posted, shared, and reshared. Members of the local media were alerted to the story and began contacting the school with requests for comments and information about the missing teacher. This once-quiet neighborhood school became the epicenter of a potential tragedy that nobody was prepared to address.

School officials, aware of my expertise in crisis communications, reached out to me for help to guide them as they tried to navigate this distressing situation.

Rule Number One Is Do No Harm

My first recommendation was that the school immediately post a statement on their social media channels for two reasons. First, posting about the missing teacher would alert more people in the community who could help in the efforts to find her. Second, other schools had already posted messages of support, and this magnified the fact that they hadn't made any statements yet, which was confusing to many people in the community.

In keeping with the first rule of crisis communications—which is to do no harm—I suggested we post the same information that local authorities were sharing. This both ensured the accuracy of the information they were making public and encouraged more members of the community to help in the search. After confirming the facts, the school posted all the relevant information, along with a dedicated tips hotline phone number, on their social media channels. These posts served the dual purpose of slowing down the volume of calls to the school while also responding to the community's desire to help.

I continued to guide the school administration through this very tense time, running interference with media, preparing communications, and thinking through the timing of messaging when it was revealed that the situation had a tragic ending.

The Golden Hour

When a crisis is unfolding, there is a short window of opportunity to address the situation and avoid or at least minimize any additional chaos that can result as employees, the media, and other members of the community seek out more information. This is the time when a holding statement, which we covered in chapter three, is needed most. While the active shooter incident was unfolding, for example, we released a statement from our CEO acknowledging the incident and promising to provide further information when available. Addressing the incident promptly allowed my team to focus on staying ahead of messaging instead of being forced to manage a multitude of calls, emails, or social media inquiries on the matter.

The same approach of putting out a simple statement at the initial stages of a crisis allowed my daughter's school to shift from reactive to proactive communications.

Unless you have made a conscious decision to maintain strategic silence—a strategy I cover in detail in chapter five—it's imperative that you address a crisis right away. Your goal should always be to get something out in front of the public within the first hour of an incident. In PR circles, this is known as the Golden Hour.

Your first communication can be a holding statement tailored to the occasion, or if you have more information to offer and can do so while following the do-no-harm rule, move forward with that. As Will Rogers famously said, you never get a second chance to make a first impression. If you don't step up and publicly face the crisis head-on during the Golden Hour, you are not only passing up an opportunity to guide the narrative, but you could also lose control of the story altogether and end up with some hard-to-repair damage to your brand.

How TYLENOL and KFC Got It Right

One of the best examples of facing a crisis head-on dates back to 1982, when Johnson & Johnson confronted a serious crisis with their TYLENOL brand of acetaminophen, the popular over-the-counter painkiller. That year, seven people in the Chicago area died after taking Extra Strength TYLENOL capsules.[3] It turned out that someone had tampered with the medicine, lacing it with cyanide, a deadly poison.

As soon as the deaths were discovered and linked to its product, TYLENOL's parent company, Johnson & Johnson, sprang into action. Without waiting for the conclusion of an investigation to determine how widespread the problem was or how the cyanide got into the capsules, Johnson & Johnson issued a recall of all thirty-one million bottles of TYLENOL that had reached stores or were in consumer hands. This recall cost the company over $100 million.

> Your goal should always be to get something out in front of the public within the first hour of an incident. In PR circles, this is known as the Golden Hour.

To warn the public not to consume any TYLENOL they had in their possession and to spread the news of the recall as quickly and widely as possible, Johnson & Johnson pulled out all the stops. They issued a series of public announcements and partnered with law enforcement, the Food and Drug Administration, and the media to get the word out. Following the investigation—it was determined that the product had been tampered with after it left the manufacturer's control—the company created new tamper-evident packaging, setting a new industry standard for safe packaging.

Johnson & Johnson's speed, transparency, and commitment to putting the good of the public before profits have earned it a stellar reputation as a trustworthy company. The TYLENOL brand of acetaminophen remains a top seller in its category today.

---

3   "TYLENOL® Tampering Incidents and Recall, 1982," Johnson & Johnson Our Story, accessed March 3, 2025, https://ourstory.jnj.com/tylenol%C2%AE-tampering-incidents-and-recall.

There's no doubt that stepping up quickly to do the right thing is the key to engendering customer trust and loyalty. Of course, not every crisis will be a matter of life and death. Most situations you encounter will be about managing your customers' expectations. In these instances, finding opportunities to inject some humor into your messaging can go a long way.

The popular fried chicken chain KFC leveraged humor to turn its reputation around by turning its signature lettered logo around.

In 2018, nearly half of KFC's nine hundred stores based in the United Kingdom had to close temporarily due to a chicken delivery delay. Finding their favorite restaurant shuttered, patrons took to social media to air their disappointment. Some even called the police, prompting one hamlet's police department to make the following post on Twitter:

> Please do not contact us about the #KFCCrisis – it is not a police matter if your favourite eatery is not serving the menu that you desire.[4]

KFC, in response to the crisis, took out several full-page ads in UK newspapers, apologizing for the chicken shortage. The ads featured an empty chicken bucket with its usual logo consisting of the letters KFC rearranged as FCK, a tongue-in-cheek expletive expressing the company's acknowledgment of the problem.

---

4   Tower Hamlets Police (@MPSTowerHam), "Please do not contact us about the #KFCCrisis – it is not a police matter if your favourite eatery is not serving the menu that you desire," Twitter (now X), February 20, 2018, https://x.com/MPSTowerHam/status/965951677105917952.

According to reports,[5] these self-deprecating ads were KFC's way of apologizing to its customers and franchise partners for the situation while also expressing how the company felt when it realized the impact the restaurant closures had on patrons. By acknowledging the issue promptly and addressing it with a humorous yet authentic apology, the chain went a long way in restoring its reputation.

How Wells Fargo and United Airlines Got It Wrong

Being slow to acknowledge a situation, on the other hand, especially if it involves wrongdoing on your company's part, can create an even bigger crisis with far-reaching implications.

In the early 2000s, complaints began to surface that Wells Fargo employees were creating fake bank and credit card accounts for existing customers without their knowledge.[6] These customers were charged fees on these accounts, resulting in damage to their credit scores and their overall financial health.

These allegations continued to surge over the next few years as Wells Fargo downplayed the extent or severity of the situation, even going as far as issuing a public statement blaming the practice on a mere handful of employees. Not only did the company maintain this false narrative for years, but it also doubled down on it. The bank issued a public statement that employees who engaged in these practices were acting on their own and that bank executives had no knowledge of or involvement in these activities. The Wells Fargo CEO

5   Jenna Amatulli, "KFC Says 'FCK' in Full-Page Ad Apologizing for Chicken Shortage," HuffPost, February 22, 2018, https://www.huffpost.com/entry/kfc-says-fck-in-full-page-ad-apologizing-for-chicken-shortage_n_5a9034b1e4b0ee6416a2adfb.

6   James Venable, "Wells Fargo: Where Did They Go Wrong?" Scholars at Harvard, accessed March 17, 2025, https://scholar.harvard.edu/files/jtv/files/wells_fargo_where_did_they_go_wrong_by_james_venable_pdf_02.pdf.

even testified under oath before Congress that the problem was caused by a few rogue employees.

The scandal came to a head in 2016 when it was disclosed that employees had opened more than 3.5 million unauthorized bank and credit card accounts using existing customers' information without their prior consent. The Wells Fargo bankers faked customer signatures, created account access PINs, and even effected money transfers between unauthorized accounts to give the impression that they were legitimate and active.

Following years of investigation, Wells Fargo ended up agreeing to pay $3 billion[7] to settle criminal and civil cases and was fined an additional $4 billion. The bank's CEO resigned, and 5,300 of its employees were fired for participating in the scheme.

Wells Fargo's initial response was the exact opposite of good crisis communications. When the bank, which was slow to acknowledge the problem in the first place, finally responded to the allegations, it tried to downplay the damage while defending the indefensible. The scandal severely damaged Wells Fargo's brand as it became an example of unethical banking practices and corporate greed.

In another infamous crisis management failure, United Airlines[8] grossly mismanaged its reaction to a 2017 viral video showing a passenger being forcibly removed from a plane. Flight attendants had asked for volunteers to give up their seats on an overbooked flight

---

7   "Wells Fargo Agrees to Pay $3 Billion to Resolve Criminal and Civil Investigations into Sales Practices Involving the Opening of Millions of Accounts Without Customer Authorization," US Department of Justice, accessed March 17, 2025, https://www. justice.gov/archives/opa/pr/wells-fargo-agrees-pay-3-billion-resolve-criminal-and-civil-investigations-sales-practices.

8   Michael Goldstein, "Biggest Travel Story of 2017: The Bumping and Beating of Dr. David Dao," *Forbes*, December 20, 2017, https://www.forbes.com/sites/michaelgoldstein/2017/12/20/biggest-travel-story-of-2017-the-bumping-and-beating-of-doctor-david-dao/.

out of Chicago O'Hare International Airport in exchange for travel vouchers. The airline needed the seats in order to make room for four staff members. When there were no volunteers, the airline randomly chose four passengers, one of whom was Dr. David Dao, a sixty-nine-year-old physician. Dr. Dao refused to leave the flight, explaining that he was scheduled to see patients the following day.

Even though the flight attendants insisted that Dr. Dao give up his seat, he steadfastly refused. The crew ended up calling in the police, who forcibly dragged the resistant Dr. Dao out of his seat, knocking him unconscious and breaking his nose and several teeth in the process. Dr. Dao also suffered a concussion. Passenger-recorded videos of the incident went viral, causing a media frenzy and public calls to boycott the airline.

United's response to the incident couldn't have been worse given the international outrage around the incident. Its CEO issued a public statement defending the airline's actions, claiming that airline personnel had followed established procedures and that Dr. Dao, by refusing to give up his seat, was responsible for what happened.

Eventually, as the airline's stock plummeted—United's stock dropped $1 billion in value in just a few days—the CEO reversed course and issued a public apology to Dr. Dao. United ended up settling a lawsuit with the doctor for a reportedly significant but undisclosed amount. The airline also revised its overbooking policies and banned the forcible removal of seated passengers.

I have no doubt that had United issued a public apology sooner and announced an action plan to prevent something like this from happening again, its brand would have recovered faster and the damage to its stock value and reputation would have been significantly mitigated.

The Strategic Pause

Along with letting the public know that you are on top of a crisis situation and expressing your compassion for those impacted, the purpose of a holding statement is to provide a moment to assess the situation holistically and buy you time before having to take further action.

Nonaction may seem counterintuitive in a crisis and is certainly not what I would often recommend. However, there are times when you should pause communications. It's human nature to want to fix things, and many people find inaction uncomfortable. But it can also be necessary, as a statement made in haste can backfire.

PAUSE TO VERIFY INFORMATION

Taking a strategic pause gives you time to check and double-check facts, make sure the information you have is accurate and complete, and decide what you want to say and how you want to say it.

Good journalists don't report something as fact unless and until they have verified it through multiple reliable sources. Sticking to this stringent protocol can be particularly challenging if people have already started posting live reports of an incident on social media. Even if it looks like these reports are credible, information that's circulated on social media is often based on rumor, innuendo, and a lack of facts. Photos and videos can be misleading when not put into context. Resist the urge to jump in too quickly or before the information has been verified through trusted sources.

During the FedEx Indianapolis shooting, my team was monitoring the horrific events as they played out on social and traditional broadcast media. Employees on the scene were posting on social media. But until we had confirmation of what happened—including how many were killed and injured, who the perpetrator was, and what the motives for the shooting were—we refrained from providing any statements until we were sure of the facts and received the go-ahead from law enforcement on the ground.

It wasn't easy to avoid answering direct questions from the media about how many were killed and injured, the identity of the shooter, and whether or not he had been a FedEx employee. The last thing we wanted was to be seen as evasive, but the worst thing we could have done was release information that was inaccurate. It helped our cause that we were transparent about the reasons we were reticent to speak too soon. By letting the reporters know that we were cooperating with the investigation and that we could not confirm or deny any details about the shooting or the victims until the authorities released this information, we showed that we were both transparent and ethical. If you're up front with the press and explain that you're erring on the side of compassion and decency, they'll understand, and that will hopefully be reflected in their reporting.

> Taking a strategic pause gives you time to check and double-check facts, make sure the information you have is accurate and complete, and decide what you want to say and how you want to say it.

It also wasn't easy to stay silent when false and misleading information was being passed around on social media, but in this situation, staying silent—at least temporarily—was the right thing to do. Not only were we heeding the do-no-harm rule of crisis communications—not interfering with the investigation or discussing sensitive matters before families were notified—but we were also ensuring that we weren't putting unverified information out there, which would later have to be corrected.

PAUSE TO GATHER RESOURCES

In some cases, it may take some time following the initial notice of an incident to reach decision-makers, bring internal stakeholders up to date, and secure resources for those in need. It's OK to take a pause to address these urgent matters.

For instance, following the Indianapolis shooting, one of our biggest priorities was getting a crisis center set up near the location so that those affected—including employees, survivors, and family members—could get much-needed information and assistance. We also needed to get a team member on the scene in Indianapolis and engage our outside PR firm to help manage communications on the ground. All of this behind-the-scenes maneuvering needed to take place before we could move forward with any real detail on how we would manage the aftermath.

PAUSE BEFORE PLACING BLAME

Before you make any statements about who is responsible for a situation, it's a good idea to take a strategic pause to make sure you are seeing the entire picture. You don't want to assume your company is innocent of all wrongdoing and issue some kind of statement denying responsibility only to have to walk that statement back later. And you certainly don't want to take responsibility for something that turns out not to be your fault at all. The best course of action is to simply state that you are conducting a thorough internal investigation and that you will share the results as soon as they become available.

A strategic pause is, by definition, temporary. The idea is to buy some time while you give yourself and your organization the necessary grace to work through what could be complex and shocking facts and issues. A strategic pause, however, should not be confused with strategic silence, where it's in everyone's best interest if you simply stay above the fray.

CHAPTER FIVE

Strategic Silence: Choosing Not to Communicate

There are times when you and your team may need to make the strategic decision to not communicate, choosing silence over engagement. Strategic silence can be beneficial when you need to let events unfold before providing any input or when there is simply no benefit to entering the conversation. In these circumstances, issuing a statement, commenting on social media posts, or providing official statements in news stories—even if you're only weighing in to correct misstatements—can do more harm than good.

Strategic silence is never easy, especially for those of us who strive in most situations to set the record straight. Sometimes, though, the choice not to communicate is the best way to protect your company and your brand.

I've already discussed in detail the need to pause from commenting while you're gathering relevant facts. But there are also situations in which you should consider staying silent indefinitely, even if you have all the facts necessary to make a public statement. The first is when the story is simply not yours to tell. The second is when you're being baited into issuing a premature or irrelevant response. And the third is when common sense dictates that you keep your thoughts, feelings, and commentary to yourself.

It's Not Your Story

At some point, you're going to find reporters clamoring for a comment from your organization regarding an event that your company may have only a peripheral connection to. My advice is to always hold back in these situations. Not every story that mentions your company requires a comment.

I had a client whose former employee was involved in a highly publicized tragedy. According to news reports, this individual caused a car accident while driving under the influence of alcohol. The accident resulted in a death.

Tragic accidents involving suspected driving-under-the-influence offenses are not uncommon, and it's rare that the ex-employer of someone charged with causing this kind of accident would be drawn into the story. This was one of those rare situations, however, in which the driver was a high-profile individual, and my client, their former employer, was a high-profile institution. The press wanted to connect the dots between the two because that made for an interesting angle that would garner attention from the public.

The story of the accident captured local headlines for days. When my client was approached by local media to confirm the driver's previous employment and provide details surrounding their departure and comments on the nature of the story, I recommended they stay silent. A simple internet search could confirm the driver's previous employment, and companies are not at liberty to discuss the details of an individual's departure. While the circumstances were certainly tragic, there was no connection between the driver, the accident, and my client, their ex-employer. Commenting on the story would provide zero benefit to my client's company.

Because my client followed my advice and ignored all requests for comments, the story eventually lost traction and faded away. In these types of situations—when you have nothing to contribute, no relevant facts to share, and no wisdom to impart—you should simply stay out of the story.

I'm not suggesting that there will never be a time for commenting on a story that isn't specifically about your company. On the contrary, you certainly want to take advantage of opportunities to showcase your expertise or promote your company's competencies in the press. You just want to take care that you consider whether speaking up will involve you in a scandal, dispute, or similar situation that does your brand more harm than good.

Say you work with an organization in either academia or the private sector that engages in a certain type of research or that is known for its expertise in a particular arena. Chances are your company is regularly asked to weigh in on stories to provide a level of expertise and a perspective that can only come from a knowledgeable source. Being quoted in a way that highlights your expertise can benefit your brand. Offering your services as a domain expert to a reporter is also a great way to solidify relationships with the press. Helping reporters out goes a long way in building important connections and mutually beneficial relationships. Reporters who know they can count on you for comments or even as a source of background information are more apt to remember your kindness and present your company in a favorable light in the future.

However, when the request is something that is divisive or highly political, or looks like the reporter is stretching a scenario to create a story where there isn't one—attempts to create the proverbial mountain out of a molehill—my advice is to stay out of it. Some examples of situations to walk away from include being asked to comment on politically polarizing matters (such as partisan legislative initiatives), fielding questions on the inevitable fallout that comes every time there's a change in political leadership, or responding to requests to weigh in on any kind of headline-grabbing story that is mired in controversy. Only agree to respond to questions that showcase your expertise in ways that uplift your brand and enhance your company's reputation.

When to Avoid Being the Local Angle

It's a local reporter's job to take what's trending nationally and find a new angle or twist to create local headlines. Typically, to turn a story local, a reporter will ask a local business to weigh in on what's going on and even speculate on how they'd handle the situation if it happened to them.

A great example of this is any news surrounding student protests taking place at specific elite universities or in certain parts of the country. A reporter who's been assigned this story will want to localize these protests to make them relevant to readers. They'll do this by asking local universities—ones that aren't experiencing student protests—to weigh in on what's happening, looking for comments on what they are planning to do should similar protests occur at their campuses.

I see little value in engaging in this type of speculation. If it is not a story directly related to something that is happening at your institution, stay out of it. That said, if there is pressure to comment, simply state in general terms what your policy is. If that policy is available on your website, don't give a direct quote at all. Instead, direct the reporter to your website. That way, you're giving the reporter information they can use without risking getting drawn into a story that isn't yours and taking a stand about something that doesn't directly concern your organization.

Don't Take the Bait

Social media is a double-edged sword when it comes to crisis communications. On the one hand, when leveraged properly, social media can be a great tool for disseminating accurate information, exhibiting thought leadership, and connecting with clients and customers. On the other hand, social media can easily become a tool of disinformation and a vehicle for pulling your organization into interactions that serve no purpose and could negatively impact your brand.

The best way to avoid the negative aspects of social media is to refrain from reacting every time someone makes a remark or statement that rubs you the wrong way. Just because someone invites you to the drama doesn't mean you have to accept the invitation. But it can be hard to stand by silently and watch people take shots at your brand and reputation.

We've all experienced situations in which posts or comments appearing on the internet have hit a nerve and we've wanted to offer a defense, a correction, or a retort. Whether the offending material is for clicks or kicks, it's important that anyone posting on behalf of your company avoids getting drawn into a no-win situation. Unless there's a compelling reason to respond—inaccurate information is spreading, a thoughtful response from a customer service rep would serve to take the issue offline, or the comment could cause a safety risk—practicing strategic silence when facing internet sensationalism is the best approach.

It is important for your organization to have social media guidelines in place. Make sure there is a clear line of distinction between what is a personal opinion and what constitutes the company's party line.

At FedEx, the social media guidelines are very specific about who is authorized to speak on behalf of the company. When it comes to their personal accounts, anyone is free to comment on whatever they want however they want, as long as they make it clear in a prominent place on their page or bio that their posts are a reflection of personal opinion and not the position of the company. My best advice to anyone in management or leadership, however, has always been to keep personal social media posts positive, upbeat, and noncontroversial. Posts follow you everywhere you go. I give this same advice to my teenage children because while their opinions will change as they mature, social media never forgets. I also advise my clients against commenting at all on sensitive situations unless and until an official statement is issued, and then they should only pass that official statement on without further commentary.

The Don't Take the Bait advice applies to more than social media, of course. It also applies to any situation in which someone is trying to coax you into saying something to fulfill their agenda. High-profile people, such as C-suite executives and celebrities, are always being goaded into speaking out of turn.

I advise my clients, many of whom occupy the C-suite or fall into the celebrity category, to keep their guard up whenever they're in public. If they're at a venue where they'll be speaking in any capacity—such as offering prepared remarks, giving a podcast interview, participating in a press conference, providing an exclusive interview, or simply making statements as they arrive at and depart from an event—I advise them to be prepared to make on-the-spot decisions on whether or not to answer the questions coming their way. I remind them that they always have a choice on whether or not to speak. My coaching for these clients is always the same. I tell them, "You control the narrative. You don't have to answer every question that's asked of you. It's OK to take time to gather your thoughts. If you have something to say, say it. And then stop talking."

I also remind them that everyone has a phone with the ability to record, so even casual conversations or comments out of context are not off the record. When you are in public, nothing is off the record. Nothing.

Not surprisingly, my clients who have taken this advice almost always manage to turn the narrative in their favor.

Read the Room

There is a time and a place for everything, which is why you need to understand how to read the room. More importantly, just because you feel it doesn't mean you should say it. Failing to understand how your words will land can make a crisis much worse for your company's reputation.

I imagine that Tony Hayward, former CEO of BP, wishes he had chosen better words when responding to questions about the 2010 Deepwater Horizon oil rig explosion in the Gulf of Mexico. The Deepwater accident caused the worst oil spill in US history and was an environmental catastrophe of epic proportions. The disaster resulted in the death of eleven workers and the spilling of millions of barrels of oil into the sea, destroying marine life and the economies of nearby communities. When asked how he was coping with the tragedy, Hayward famously responded, "I'd like my life back." This seemingly dismissive comment in the face of a crisis that saw loss of life and had huge implications for the environment and Gulf Coast economies fueled public outrage. Even though he followed up the thoughtless remarks with a public apology,[9] the damage was done. He was replaced as CEO within weeks.

Coming off as insensitive or clueless is never a good look for a company spokesperson. I'm sure the seventy thousand attendees of the 2024 Burning Man festival[10] who found themselves stranded in the Nevada desert after heavy rains turned their campgrounds into mud were not amused when the event CEO wondered why everyone was making "such a fuss." Marian Goodell was definitely not reading the room when she went on national television with comments such as, "There is no cause to panic" and "We do not see this as an evacuation situation," as festivalgoers whose campgrounds were buried in mud and whose vehicles were immobilized were forced to trudge through the near-impassable muck on foot for up to six miles to reach civilization.

It's human nature to have strong emotions during and following a crisis event, and it's not unusual for the people in charge to feel defensive when things don't go their way. But that doesn't mean it's ever a good idea to express those sentiments publicly. Don't make an already difficult situation worse by being unprepared to handle public statements or questions. Draft responses to expected questions in advance and stick to those statements. Any time a spokesperson goes off script, especially when they're already in an uncomfortable situation or aren't used to being in front of the press, the results can be detrimental. If you have concerns that the executive representing your company isn't going to do well in a stressful situation, have a

---

9   "BP CEO Apologizes for 'Thoughtless' Oil Spill Comment," *Reuters*, June 1, 2010, https://www.reuters.com/article/business/environment/ bp-ceo-apologizes-for-thoughtless-oil-spill-comment-idUSTRE6515NQ.

10   "Burning Man Crowd Stuck at Muddy Venue, but There's No Cause for Panic, CEO Says," NBC News, September 3, 2023, https://www.nbcnews.com/pop-culture/pop-culture-news/ burning-man-crowd-stuck-muddy-venue-no-cause-panic-ceo-says-rcna103217.

trained spokesperson handle the public appearances instead. You can always have a prepared statement from the CEO to accompany your PR and media efforts.

When the Silence Is Deafening

So far in this chapter, I've been talking about strategic silence—with an emphasis on the word *strategic*. The idea of strategic silence is to consciously and thoughtfully choose to let the narrative take shape without your input. As we've established, it's wise to consider employing this strategy when speaking up would either serve no useful purpose or when it would do more harm than good.

But never confuse the purposeful employment of strategic silence with staying quiet because you are not prepared or you're hoping that a situation will simply go away, especially if your company caused the situation.

Facebook remained silent for five days in 2018[11] after first learning that data from tens of millions of users—it was eventually determined to have been eighty-seven million—had been misused by British political consulting firm Cambridge Analytica in political campaigns. When CEO Mark Zuckerberg finally made a statement, his apology was viewed as weak, causing several undesired consequences. The public created #DeleteFacebook, a hashtag that trended worldwide. Mark Zuckerberg was called upon to testify at con-

> The idea of strategic silence is to consciously and thoughtfully choose to let the narrative take shape without your input.

---

11   Julie Carrie Wong, "Mark Zuckerberg Apologises for Facebook's 'Mistakes' over Cambridge Analytica," *The Guardian*, March 22, 2018, https://www.theguardian.com/technology/2018/mar/21/mark-zuckerberg-response-facebook-cambridge-analytica.

gressional hearings, and the social media platform was fined $5 billion[12] by the Federal Trade Commission, as well as subjected to sweeping new privacy restrictions. Speaking up sooner would not have eliminated all of these outcomes, but it certainly would have helped mitigate some of the long-term damage to the brand.

There have always been pros and cons to utilizing a spokesperson to represent your brand. From A-list celebrities to spokespeople created by the brand, anytime you link your brand's reputation to a particular person, you are taking a risk. People are human, and there is always the potential that a scandal will occur.

Just hear the name Kanye West and you can't help but think about the 2009 Taylor Swift MTV Music Video Awards incident and the backlash he's received[13] from years of making public remarks considered offensive by different ethnic groups. It's also hard to forget that his reputation for controversy has caused him to be dropped from his affiliation with some major brands, such as adidas and Balenciaga, making him a pariah in celebrity endorsement circles. Tiger Woods's reputation as one of the greatest golfers of all time has been overshadowed by his relationship trials, including his highly publicized infidelities, and reports of alcohol and substance abuse. Woods lost several endorsement deals[14] for brands including Gatorade, Gillette, Accenture, and AT&T. Seven-time Tour de France winner and cancer

12   "FTC Imposes $5 Billion Penalty and Sweeping New Privacy Restrictions on Facebook," Federal Trade Commission, July 24, 2019, https://www.ftc.gov/news-events/news/press-releases/2019/07/ftc-imposes-5-billion-penalty-sweeping-new-privacy-restrictions-facebook.

13   Anna Chan, Rania Aniftos, Hannah Dailey, and Starr Bowenbank, "A Timeline of the Consequences Ye Has Faced for His 'WLM' Shirts & Antisemitic Hate Speech," Billboard, February 12, 2025, https://www.billboard.com/lists/kanye-west-hate-speech-consequences-timeline/.

14   "The Tiger Woods Scandal Forced Companies to Think Twice About Risky Endorsers," Harvard Business Review, accessed March 10, 2025, https://hbr.org/2014/03/the-tiger-woods-scandal-made-companies-think-twice-about-risky-endorsers.

survivor Lance Armstrong will forever be remembered for one of the biggest doping scandals in sports, which resulted in his being dropped from partnerships[15] with brands such as Nike, Trek Bicycle Corporation, Anheuser-Busch, and Oakley, to name just a few.

While not all celebrity ties to your brand will turn out badly, when they do, you need to distance your brand as quickly as possible to minimize brand risk.

Jared Fogle became a household name after being featured for years in Subway advertisements as the guy who lost weight eating Subway sandwiches. After Fogle was charged and convicted of child exploitation, Subway waited weeks before cutting ties with him. This delay caused a significant public backlash, with the damage from the way Subway handled (or didn't handle) the scandal leading to long-term impacts, including declining franchise sales and restrictions on subsequent marketing efforts.[16]

It is important to step up, say something, and take action whenever your company is confronted with a situation that is harming your brand, regardless of whether the incident was caused by your company, directly reflects on your company, or happened while you were the leader. Even if you say very little more than acknowledging the issue and pledging to find out more, say *something*.

In January 2025, Mayor Karen Bass faced significant criticism for her absence during the beginning of Los Angeles's devastating wildfires. Bass was attending a scheduled event in Ghana when the fires erupted, leading to public outcry over her absence. Although she returned as quickly as possible, when she landed at Los Angeles Inter-

---

15   Allan Dowd, "Armstrong Loses Eight Sponsors in a Day," CNBC, October 18, 2012, https://www.cnbc.com/2012/10/18/armstrong-loses-eight-sponsors-in-a-day.html.

16   Jonah Sachs, "Subway's Silence over the Jared Fogle Fiasco Leaves a Bad Taste," *The Guardian*, August 27, 2015, https://www.theguardian.com/sustainable-business/2015/aug/27/subway-jared-fogle-child-abuse-obesity-marketing.

national Airport, she was met with reporters expecting to hear from the city's leader about why she had left the country with the wildfire threat hanging over the city and what she was doing to address the crisis in light of recent budget cuts to the Los Angeles Fire Department. However, the mayor declined to answer any questions and, ignoring reporters as she made her way out of the airport, refused to say anything at all. This refusal to engage with the media—which was captured on video—intensified the backlash, with critics accusing her of neglecting her duties and lacking transparency.[17] The combination of her absence, her silence, and her undefended policy decisions led to widespread dissatisfaction and calls for accountability.

This is a great example of where being prepared could have paid off. My philosophy and the advice I share with my clients is to be prepared with something to say, say it, and then stop talking. Much of the negative public scrutiny the mayor endured could have been avoided had she been properly prepared by her communications staff. My advice to her would have been to face any reporters directly and explain that she had returned as quickly as possible and that she had been in constant contact with staff on the ground during her long flight home. I'd have advised her to explain that she would be holding a press conference soon to answer questions fully. Then, she could have thanked them for their patience and left.

Even when you don't have all of the answers, making the choice to say something over staying silent can make all of the difference.

---

17   Steve Large and Richard Ramos, "LA Mayor Karen Bass Awkwardly
       Ignores Questions from Reporter About California Fires," CBS News,
       January 10, 2025, https://www.cbsnews.com/sacramento/news/
       la-mayor-karen-bass-ignores-questions-about-california-fires/.

CHAPTER SIX

Document Everything—Always

One of the cornerstones of effective crisis communications is documentation. Carefully and completely documenting what transpires during and immediately after a crisis helps inform actions in real time. And the records you keep regarding how the crisis was handled and the issues encountered will be of immense value if and when a similar incident is encountered in the future.

When it comes to deciding how detailed to get in your crisis documentation, I believe in erring on the side of granularity. In fact, when it comes to crisis management and communications, there's no such thing as too much documentation.

If you observe it, hear it, or read it and it is relevant to the crisis you're facing, write it down. This pertains to formal internal and external statements, meeting notes, emails, situation reports, and anything else that pertains to the incident.

Setting Up a Crisis Documentation Infrastructure

The kind and level of resources you'll need to pour into your documentation efforts is going to depend on the size of your organization and the nature of your crisis.

For example, if you run a midsize manufacturing company that's dealing with an unanticipated supply chain interruption, you'll want to make sure that at least one individual from each relevant internal department—such as receiving and warehousing, production, shipping, sales, marketing, customer service, and human resources—documents what is happening in the area they oversee. Supply chain issues can interrupt operations, affect workers' livelihoods, and impact customers waiting for and expecting needed items. So, how communications flow in real time, what kinds of challenges arise, and how those challenges are handled can impact your overall operations.

> When it comes to crisis management and communications, there's no such thing as too much documentation.

Tracking what occurs and recording things in writing will not only help you retain visibility into all aspects of the business as you manage the crisis, but they will also help inform how you handle future situations. To help facilitate the documentation process, I recommend employing some kind of file-sharing system—such as Google Docs, SharePoint, or a folder in Teams—where anyone in your organization with information to share can easily upload memos and reports.

If you're managing the crisis communications for a large company, there are going to be more people involved and more moving pieces to keep track of, making documentation challenging. For big corporations or institutions, I recommend appointing someone to manage crisis and response documentation. This person's role is to collect information from the involved parties and create a company repository for all crisis-related matters. This is the place where everyone involved with the crisis will forward their call notes, emails, and any other information relevant to the situation, such as police reports or insurance documents.

If you've set up a war room or some other centralized crisis management center, it's a good idea to appoint a person whose job will be to keep accurate minutes of meetings and develop situation reports. To ensure accuracy, you can always record calls and meetings and have the records transcribed with the assistance of AI, but you still need a designated lead to manage the process and edit and organize the information so it's both useful and easy to locate.

What to Share and What to Protect

Keeping detailed records doesn't mean that all the information gathered will be disclosed or disseminated in a future incident report—I've provided an incident report template below—or a media statement. In fact, much of the information you gather may turn out to be irrelevant to managing the crisis or informing future actions. The reason I support thorough notetaking and recordkeeping is to ensure you have accurate records of meetings and events from which you can retrieve important information for reports, checklists, and statements. You don't always know what information may be useful or even necessary in the future, which is why it's always best to err on the side of as much detail as possible. At some point, you may need to refer back to those detailed records to address legal or compliance questions that may arise in lawsuits or outside investigations after the fact.

Of course, private, confidential, and privileged information needs to remain secure and out of unauthorized hands. Information that needs to be protected could include the identities of victims or suspects in connection with a crime—particularly if there is an ongoing investigation or family members have yet to be notified—as well as any information that could fall under the category of confidential business intelligence. It's important that any private conversations—such as those with law enforcement, your own security team, city and county officials, or anyone who is relaying information to you that is not yet public or that you have not been given permission to release in a statement or share beyond a close circle of people—remain secure.

The infrastructure I'm encouraging you to establish around crisis documentation may seem excessive. While it could be tempting to dismiss this recommendation as one of those so-called best practices that experts advocate but nobody actually follows, I can tell you from my experience that documentation is crucial to your role as an effective crisis communications lead.

Bracing for Another Memphis Snowstorm

A perfect example of just how important thoroughly documenting a crisis can be happened a few months after I assumed the role of chief marketing and communications officer at the University of Memphis.

As someone who was born and raised in Tennessee, I can say with authority that Southerners don't do winter very well. Nobody panics like a Southerner facing a snowstorm. At the first announcement that temperatures are going to dip below freezing with a chance of snow or ice, there's a mad rush to stock up on staples, such as eggs, bread, and milk.

While we Southerners might love the idea of a winter wonderland—the kind you see in those Hallmark Christmas movies—what we usually end up with after just a few inches of snow or ice accumulation is an infrastructure nightmare. Despite law enforcement's pleas to stay home, too many people still venture out on the roadways, under the illusion that they understand how to drive in inclement weather.

When Memphis was predicted to experience four to six inches of snow, I already knew what to do because I had a road map. Honestly, describing the document as a road map doesn't do justice to the robust, twenty-one-page, no-stone-left-unturned, detailed postcrisis report—complete with checklists and steps on how to anticipate, prepare for, and manage every winter weather-related issue that could possibly impact the university campus, the students, and the faculty and staff.

WHAT'S PAST IS PROLOGUE

Why did I have this detailed document? Because the year before, Memphis had experienced a winter storm that dropped six inches of snow on the city and surrounding areas. The entire metro area had shut down. Power had been lost in many parts of the city, and a boil-water order had been put in place.

The University of Memphis, whose main campus is located on sixteen hundred acres in the heart of the city, was severely impacted by the city's 2024 storm-related infrastructure problems. Students were stuck in their campus dorms. Many staff and faculty members were unable to get to campus given the city's road conditions, and even the campus facilities management staff met challenges attempting to clear areas on campus and repair frozen-pipe damage. Several buildings flooded when pipes burst, and some structures became unsafe.

Given the weather-induced challenges affecting the city, the university's crisis management team worked through how to address emergent needs and documented everything that was happening in detail.

More importantly, once things were back to normal, they held a postmortem meeting to review the documentation, add lessons learned, and provide guidance for future weather-related incidents. These documents not only spell out the details of storm preparation and recovery efforts, but they also provide detailed process improvements to ensure that we get through future storms safely and with minimal disruptions to campus life and infrastructure. As the person who subsequently stepped into the role of managing the university's crisis communications, I am thankful for the thoroughness and clarity of this report. It's an invaluable tool I can refer to as we all prepare for a potential worst-case weather scenario. This team left things better for the next time and the next team.

Structure of a Postcrisis Report

In my experience, the university's aptly named After Action Report (AAR) represents the gold standard of what a postcrisis management report should look like. Not only does the AAR focus on what happened but it also addresses why things happened so that the insights contained in the report will help guide decision-makers in the future. It sets forth what worked, what didn't work, and what concrete steps can be taken for improvement. Perhaps most importantly, by demonstrating transparency and refusing to play the blame game, the report's authors create a safe space for participants and observers to be forthcoming with their observations, suggestions, and feedback.

Even though every crisis is different—so it only stands to reason that every incident report will be different—the following outline can help you develop your own incident reports and checklists.

OUTLINE FOR AN INCIDENT/ SITUATION REPORT

1. **Description of the Incident**

   - Provide an overview of the event, including the date/time of when the incident began and ended, location(s), and sequence of events.

   - List the people involved, including who was in charge of the operation and the key individuals providing crisis response oversight. Names and titles are important because, while people may come and go from positions, the need for the roles remains the same.

   - Briefly explain what occurred and what the warning signs were, if any. Describe any pre-incident preparations, if applicable. For example, preparations for a weather event.

2. **Immediate Actions Taken**

   - Describe the actions taken within the first few hours of the incident. Were emergency services called? Were emergency communications/alerts distributed? Include information about the departments engaged and their roles.

   - Were any challenges encountered? What were they? Were they resolved? If so, how?

3. **Impact Assessment/Property Damage Report**

   - Provide the details of damage to people, property, or business operations. Outline plans for remediation, including costs.

   - Provide insights into whether anything could have been done to prevent or mitigate the damage, if applicable.

4. **Personal Injuries Report**

   - Was anyone injured during the event? Provide details.

- How were injuries addressed?

5. **Communications Report**

- Describe internal communications efforts. What channels, who led the communications, and when/how often? List the meetings held and include minutes and recordings, emails, phone alerts, intranet messages, etc.

- Describe external communications efforts. How were messages disseminated and by whom? Include all public-facing communications, such as the company website, emails, statements, press releases, press conferences, media interviews, and social media posts and replies/monitoring.

- Provide an outcomes analysis detailing what was effective and what improvements can be made for the future.

6. **Follow-Up Actions**

- Outline what safety improvements, operational enhancements, or new policies should be addressed as a result.

- Determine and assign departments responsible for overseeing corrective actions.

- Capture what went right. Outline the actions or learnings that should be taken into consideration for the next incident or event.

Depending on the nature of the crisis and the size of your operations, an activity report covering these matters can end up being anywhere from just a few pages to hundreds of pages that include detailed attachments and exhibits. How you structure the report and how much information you include will depend on both circumstances and resources.

As you put your own postcrisis report together, think about the importance of the report for the next person. In other words, do what my colleagues here at the university did and ask yourself, "What do I know now that I wish I'd known before?"

Incident or Situation Reports

Sometimes, while a crisis is still unfolding and you're in the middle of managing the situation, you may want to create and disseminate single-topic situation reports. I've found these types of reports beneficial for keeping certain stakeholders apprised of what's happening, including any new developments. Creating these types of situation reports for FedEx leadership proved extremely useful during the Indianapolis shooter crisis, for example. My team was able to keep senior leadership apprised of new developments without having to stop what we were doing to respond to emails and phone calls. Sometimes, the reports would be a page or two long, and other times, they might simply say that there were no changes to the previous report. By creating these short situation reports on a regular cadence, leadership could rest assured that they were staying on top of a very fluid situation and weren't being left in the dark with respect to important matters.

At times, the crisis you're dealing with will only require a one- or two-page incident report because the situation itself is short-lived or not overly complex. For instance, if one of your facilities is evacuated due to a suspected gas leak and it's determined in short order that it was a false alarm, allowing you to resume normal operations, an incident report is all that you'd need to document the crisis.

I've provided an incident report template below. You'll see that there are many similarities between an AAR and a situation report as far as potential topics to include. The differences are that a situation report is restricted to a specific period—each report has a date and a time on it—or incident and is intended to inform stakeholders of what's going on in near real time. And while an AAR is a tool for postcrisis reviews and management, as discussed in detail in chapter nine, a situation report is meant to offer a snapshot of what's happening in real time. If you think of an AAR as a book, a situation report might be one of its chapters or even a section of one of its chapters. The recipient should be able to quickly glance through the situation report and have a good understanding of what has occurred in the short period covered in the report. Be sure to include any communications disseminated so that those receiving them have the exact language to use if they are asked questions or need to share information with their team members.

TEMPLATE FOR AN INCIDENT/ SITUATION REPORT

1. **Basic Information**
   - **Report date and time:** (when the report is being written)
   - **Incident date and time:** (when the incident occurred)
   - **Location:** (where the incident happened)
   - **Incident type:** (accident, injury, security breach, property damage, misconduct, etc.)

2. **Description of the Incident**
   - **Summary:** (brief overview of what happened)
   - **Detailed account:** (sequence of events leading to the incident)
   - **People involved:** (names, roles, and involvement of employees, customers, witnesses, or third parties)
   - **Conditions and contributing factors:** (weather, equipment failure, human error, policy violations, etc.)

3. **Immediate Actions Taken**
   - **Response measures:** (first aid, security intervention, containment efforts, etc.)
   - **Emergency services contacted:** (if applicable, including police, fire department, medical personnel, etc.)
   - **Notifications:** (who was informed—supervisors, management, human resources, legal, external authorities, etc.)

4. **Communications**
   - **Holding statement**
   - **Internal statements/communications**
   - **Media statement**

5. **Impact Assessment**
   - **Injuries/damage:** (description of any harm to people, property, or business operations)
   - **Business disruption:** (how the incident affected daily operations)
   - **Financial loss (if applicable):** (costs related to damage, repairs, or legal issues)

6. **Follow-Up Actions and Resolution**
   - **Corrective measures implemented:** (safety improvements, retraining, new policies, etc.)
   - **Business continuity:** (estimated time for operations to return to normal)
   - **Ongoing investigations:** (if further inquiry is needed, outline of next steps)
   - **Responsible departments:** (who will oversee corrective actions)
   - **Next report date/time**

Not every element of this template is going to be required for every report. The idea is to look at who your intended audience is and ask yourself what the recipient wants or needs to know about this particular incident.

CHAPTER
SEVEN

Seeking Out and Accepting Help

If this book is serving as your guide, before you confront your first crisis as communications lead, you have already put together a solid crisis response team, conducted regular practice drills, and prepared holding statements and checklists as part of your crisis communications plan. You'll have covered your bases by ensuring enough redundancies in your team functions that you're confident that crucial positions will be filled even if core team members are unavailable or need temporary respite.

In a perfect world, setting up this type of infrastructure would mean having the resources you need to manage whatever situations arise.

The thing is, I've yet to confront a crisis where everything goes as planned.

The Importance of Recognizing Limitations

I hope I haven't left you with the impression that as a crisis communications lead, you're expected to be able to handle every crisis on your own and be all things to all people. Because you're not. Crisis communications is a team effort, and those of us who have many years of experience never hesitate to call in reinforcements when necessary. Asking for help is not a sign of weakness; it's a sign of smart leadership. Too often, leaders are unwilling or even afraid to ask for help. Maybe because they are wary of appearing unqualified or inexperienced, or they simply don't want to appear weak. While this kind of thinking is counterproductive in every leadership scenario, it can be dangerous when it comes to crisis management and communications. Depending on the crisis, people's lives, property, or livelihoods might be at stake. Often, time is of the essence in addressing a crisis situation properly.

> Asking for help is not a sign of weakness; it's a sign of smart leadership.

You simply can't afford to hold back on getting the resources you need at the moment you need them. When you're in the midst of a crisis, it is time to put your ego aside and seek out the help you need.

Tapping into Organizational Resources

When you are entering a crisis situation with many moving parts and things are happening quickly, it's never a sign of weakness to ask for additional resources beyond your own crisis team. Your job is to manage the situation for the best outcomes possible for your people, your organization, and your brand.

Good leadership in a crisis is not only about recognizing when you need help; it's also about knowing how to secure the help you need. For instance, if your designated scribe is out and there's nobody else on your team available to sit in on meetings and fulfill this function, bring in someone from another department. If you've got a solid plan in place, almost anyone should be able to take over the scribe function.

You may also need to leverage the contacts of another department to facilitate vital crisis communications activities. During times of crisis, barriers often need to be broken, and silos may need to be dissolved. Understand where and how you can leverage internal resources when you need them. And if your organization can't provide the resources you need to effectively manage the crisis, be prepared to seek outside help.

Tapping into Resources Outside Your Organization

Regardless of how robust a communications team you've established in your organization, there is always a possibility that you're going to need additional resources outside of your company.

You'd be hard-pressed to find a company more supportive of its internal communications teams than FedEx. The company leadership has a deep understanding of how important it is to communicate often and effectively with its worldwide network of team members, its customers around the globe, and its thousands of shareholders.

This support is particularly apparent during crisis situations in which FedEx supports a team dedicated to crisis communications. But even with all this backing, and despite the abundance of internal resources I could access at any given moment as vice president of global communications, there were instances when I needed to look outside the company for help.

During the Indianapolis shooting incident and its immediate aftermath, it became apparent that we were going to need someone on location in Indianapolis who could coordinate FedEx's response with law enforcement and all the involved local and state government officials while simultaneously managing local, state, and national media. This was a big job that required assigning a dedicated leader to be on-site. We sent a communications leader to manage the situation and serve as a company spokesperson. Even with the ability to deploy internal resources and a strong crisis communications plan, the situation required expertise and resources beyond what I could pull together from within the company.

I turned to our PR firm, Edelman, to provide guidance based on its breadth of experience in crisis communications. Knowing that I had a trusted partner who could seamlessly jump in to manage immediate needs or, more importantly, think ahead freed me up to focus my attention on meeting the immediate needs of our affected staff and on facilitating communications with our global employees and customers. I needed someone to think ahead and clear the path as my team worked on immediate needs. Having the team at Edelman connect us with other clients who had been through similar workplace shooting incidents was incredibly helpful. They provided a resource that we likely wouldn't have thought of and certainly wouldn't have been able to connect with quickly. Edelman's assistance was truly invaluable.

Similarly, as an outside crisis communications consultant, I was able to provide assistance to my daughter's school administrators during their crisis. When it became apparent that the missing teacher had indeed been kidnapped, the school's administrators, who were aware of my background in crisis management, asked for my help. As a concerned parent and member of their community who happened to also be an expert in crisis communications, I was able to immediately provide the assistance they needed, which included advising them on social media, fielding press inquiries, and communicating with staff, parents, and the community.

Preselecting Your Outside Assistance

If it turns out that you need outside assistance, things will move more smoothly if you've preselected a crisis communications management expert or firm before you are faced with an actual crisis. My daughter's school was quickly able to access a crisis communications professional in their own community to assist. This was a deeply personal crisis for everyone at the school, which made the situation emotionally charged, and I provided an outside perspective. While it impacted me because it was simply the most horrible situation, I didn't have personal connections, which allowed me to focus on the tasks in front of us.

Similarly, being able to call Edelman and knowing I had the support I needed during the events in Indianapolis made all the difference in FedEx's ability to stay on top of the situation and respond appropriately to fast-moving events.

You don't want to put yourself or your staff in the position of looking around for help when you're already in a serious situation. You should think through the type of help you could need and how and where you're going to be able to get it well before you need it.

Sometimes, especially if you're managing the crisis communications of a larger company, it makes sense to bring in a PR firm on retainer. An experienced consultant can assess your operations and provide strategic input regarding your internal controls and procedures, your overall crisis communications plan, and how well your organization is staffed to manage different types of scenarios. They also have staff who can step in and work alongside your team when necessary. Having an outside consultant can be especially beneficial if you're new to an organization and could use some help looking around corners to identify vulnerabilities. Because a consultant brings an outsider's perspective, they don't have the same personal stake in reaching certain conclusions that internal team members might have.

And being able to call on a firm you've already established a relationship with and that knows your company and your brand during a crisis can be a huge benefit.

Of course, not every business is going to need—let alone be able to budget for—a large global communications firm. Having even a small agency or consultant on retainer can be a big financial outlay—one that small and midsize companies may not be able to prioritize. But because there will come a time, regardless of your organization's size or the magnitude of the crisis you face, when being able to call in outside help is going to be immensely beneficial, knowing who to call in those moments can make all the difference.

Even if you're a one-person shop, there's nothing stopping you from doing some research and starting conversations with local agencies or crisis communications consultants to determine who would be the best fit in case you need their help. You don't want to find yourself doing Google searches for a PR consultant when you're already trying to manage a crisis. You'll end up having to hire whoever answers the phone and paying whatever rate they're offering at that time. You're much better off expending the effort to connect with someone you can call in an emergency.

If your company does not have the funds to retain or hire outside help, don't undervalue the strength of your network. Is there someone you know who has been through a crisis situation and who would be willing to answer questions? Do you have a trusted colleague or former colleague who could be your sounding board as you think through the best way to approach a situation? Could you work it out with a small firm or consultant to only pay when you activate their services in a crisis? I cannot overstate the value of thinking through your options in advance of any issue or crisis.

Practice makes permanent for the day you have to put these ideas, thoughts, and plans into motion.

The Power of Networking

No matter how experienced you might be or how well staffed your crisis communications department is, at some point, you're going to encounter a case of first impression. When that happens, the best course of action is to work your connections to find someone who's dealt with that type of situation before. From my own experience, I'm confident in saying that anyone who's faced a similar crisis will be willing to lend advice and support.

As the Indianapolis situation was unfolding, my team at Edelman asked whether we wanted to speak to someone at Molson Coors, which had experienced an active shooter incident the previous year. It was easy to answer yes because I wanted to speak with someone who had been through the same type of situation. I wasn't sure what type of advice I was seeking, but I knew that talking to another crisis communications professional at a large company that commanded a global spotlight would be helpful as I began to navigate a similar path. So, Edelman connected my boss and me with Molson Coors's crisis communications lead.

I can't emphasize enough the value of being able to tap into the knowledge and experience of someone who had managed a large company's communications through a similar scenario. My counterpart at Molson Coors shared what he had done, what he had learned, and things he wished he had known before. He even connected my leadership team with a nonprofit organization that could help us easily set up a fund for the victims' families.

I'll forever be grateful to the Edelman team and Molson Coors for their advice and assistance. No communications leader will ever know exactly how to handle every situation they'll confront in their career. That's why it's always a good idea to connect with other crisis communications professionals in your area and your industry. You never know when you'll need to pick someone's brain or be called upon yourself to lend a hand to a colleague or associate facing unfamiliar terrain.

You don't need a resource such as a large PR firm, however, to find a communications expert to connect with. You can often find someone by networking within your existing personal relationships and professional contacts.

Tell your friends you're looking to meet a crisis communications expert to seek advice and ask questions. Maybe someone has a partner or a relative in PR. If you serve on a board, ask your fellow board members for names of PR professionals you can meet. Ask around at a parents' association meeting or your book club. Until you start inquiring, you'll never know who within your current sphere can either help you out themselves or connect you with someone else who is able to provide assistance.

Several years before the teacher at my daughter's school went missing, I received a call from the school head when he was searching for a director of communications. We discussed what skills he should look for in a candidate. Specifically, he asked if finding a candidate with deep crisis communications experience was important. I shared that it is always good to have that type of experience on staff, but it is often hard to come by. I recommended he hire someone with a well-rounded skill set, someone who could handle all the school's communications needs. And I advised him to do two things if and when he encountered a crisis. First, I told him, he should call his lawyer. And second, I said, he should call me.

A few years later, the kindergarten teacher went missing, and the school called me, as advised. As the team worked through the crisis communications efforts, each of us called people in our networks to seek advice or ask specific questions. I made calls to members of my network, having spent so many years at FedEx and in the Memphis media community. We utilized the alumni and parents' networks to seek the advice we needed. One of the people in the meeting had previously worked at a large hospital that had dealt with crises in that community on a regular basis. She called her former boss at the hospital, tapping into her network for advice as well.

It really did take a village to manage the school's crisis. Thankfully, the school's management team knew how to pull out all the stops to work their networks and get the help they needed.

Accepting Help—Even When You Don't Need It

One of the most difficult things to remember as you navigate the complexities of crisis communications is that you don't own the crisis.

Whatever is happening to your organization is happening to a lot of people. Your leadership, your employees, your customers, and your community are also feeling the effects of the crisis. And many of them are going to want to help.

Your first instinct might be to refuse all offers of help that aren't immediately needed. Chances are you're going to feel like you already have enough to do, and taking the time and effort to think of ways for others to participate can feel like a burden.

I invite you to look at your role through a different lens. Instead of the orientation that your job is limited to crisis communications, think of it as brand protection or even brand enhancement. Everyone would be better off if crises could be averted altogether. But when they can't, there is absolutely nothing wrong with finding opportunities to identify positive ways for people to help. If you can create a pathway for others to lend support, that's even better.

People want to feel as though they're contributing to the solution, that they are part of something meaningful. This is especially true in situations such as the Indianapolis shooting, where FedEx team members all over the country and the world wanted to do something to show their support for and solidarity with the victims and their families.

Creating the magnetized black ribbons emblazoned with "Indy" for FedEx vehicles was a labor of love for the individual who first came up with the idea and the scores of people throughout the company who helped them realize this vision in record time. Not only did the team of people who designed, printed, and distributed the ribbons within just a few days of the incident feel as though they were part of something greater than themselves, but every single team member who drove a FedEx vehicle displaying that ribbon felt pride to stand with their team members at that moment. It was a sense of good triumphing over evil, and we all felt it—everyone at FedEx from the CEO to the dispatchers and package handlers and drivers. I feel it to this day: #FedExStrong.

It's best not to assume that it's only your internal stakeholders who want to help. There was an overwhelming outpouring of support from the greater Indianapolis community following the tragedy. For instance, a hotel near the FedEx facility donated space for victims, families, and authorities to gather, and a local Domino's Pizza provided food.

If people want to help, do your best to offer a way for them to contribute. Whether it's a blood drive, establishing a donations portal, or some way to display solidarity with those in need, with a little ingenuity and a lot of empathy, you and your team will find a way to allow those impacted in a crisis to share in the healing process.

CHAPTER
EIGHT

Leading with Your Head and Your Heart

Leadership is a choice. If you decide to pursue a leadership role, it is a choice you make every day. And some days, that choice will be harder than others, especially during a crisis. When leading during a crisis, you are responsible for managing the messaging that protects your organization and its people, brand, and reputation. But you're also taking on the responsibility of looking after the physical and emotional safety of the members of your team while guiding their development as crisis communicators.

This means that not only are you handling all the usual communications challenges—timeliness and accuracy of messaging, discernment regarding tone and delivery, and juggling competing priorities—but you and your team must also do all this while responding to rapid-fire issues that constantly arise during an emergency. Someone once called crisis communicators the Ginger Rogers of PR—a reference to the fact that 1940s movie star Ginger Rogers danced all the same steps as her famed partner Fred Astaire, except she danced them backward and in high heels.

The built-in urgencies and accompanying stress of crisis communications create unique challenges for anyone leading a crisis communications team. These include knowing the difference between stepping in when needed and micromanaging when not, dealing with the dangers of stress and burnout (both your teams' and your own), and understanding the very real repercussions of FOMO in the workplace, as discussed in depth later in this chapter.

While not all of these challenges may be apparent at the beginning of a crisis, my experience has been that the more complex, drawn-out, and multilayered the crisis, the greater the toll it will take on you and your team.

The Perils of Micromanaging

If you're attracted to this high-stakes profession, you're probably the type of person who likes to roll up your sleeves and dig into the work. This hands-on approach has an upside because it means you're always ready, willing, and able to jump in when necessary. In fact, this is where you feel most alive and most useful, and it is likely why you keep coming back for more. There's a potential downside, however, of being too hands-on as a leader. You risk being viewed as a micromanager who is robbing your team members of their opportunities to participate and grow.

A large part of crisis communications is performing under pressure when time is of the essence and there is little margin for error. As a crisis team leader, you're going to have to find the right balance that works with your specific team, recognizing their strengths while also acknowledging their weaknesses and, just as important, their potential. Too little oversight and you risk damage to your brand or even the possibility of exacerbating a crisis. Too much oversight and you could end up eroding the confidence and effectiveness of your team members. Think of yourself as the attending surgeon in an operating room. At some point, you have to turn the scalpel over to the surgical resident. But if the operation is particularly complex, with the patient's life at stake, you may not feel comfortable relinquishing the most difficult part of the procedure. There will be better opportunities for a teaching moment when the stakes are not so high.

The reality is that there are times when, as the leader, you simply have to do the heavy lifting. This could mean crafting particularly sensitive statements, managing communications with senior management, or dealing with the press concerning delicate matters. In certain high-profile situations, regardless of complexity, you may determine it's not in the best interest of the company to relinquish control of a matter to your team members. As much as you want to be a mentor and coach who encourages growth and opportunities by allowing team members to take a stab at crafting a message or triaging the tasks ahead, there will be times when you are the only one who has the experience and instincts to produce the best response to a certain event or situation.

There's no right or wrong answer here. The goal is to be mindful of your obligations, both to your company and to the team members you lead, and take the best course of action under the circumstances. Just keep in mind that you must give people a chance to prove themselves if you expect them to grow.

To be a good leader in a crisis, you have to be flexible and adaptable. In fact, your whole team has to be able to juggle multiple tasks and adapt to changing priorities and responsibilities as they present themselves. I was reminded of this recently.

Just a few weeks into my role at the university, I had several sensitive matters cross my desk that were issues that could have turned into crises. No amount of previous experience gave me insights into the background of the people or the institution. I needed information from someone trustworthy.

I am fortunate to have a director of communications who has been here longer than anyone else on the team. He is someone that I can trust to be thorough and meticulous, as well as fast. This director quickly became my trusted go-to for all urgent and confidential matters.

Since taking on this role, I have spent a good deal of time and effort building a team that is able to handle unsettling situations, especially ones that require thoughtful inquiries, precision messaging, and rapid responses. Recently, we faced a situation that needed quick action and communication with the entire faculty and staff. In these types of situations, my director of communications is my go-to person. As it turned out, during the height of the information crunch, my director was home with a sick child. I took the director's absence as an opportunity to grow the rest of the team in real time. I approached the assistant director, brought her up to speed on what was going on, and explained that the director was unavailable and that I needed her help. Without skipping a beat, she responded, "Great! Hand it over."

She was trained, she was ready, and she displayed the competence and confidence that convinced me that she was up to the challenge. She immediately got to work, bringing in another communications specialist so the three of us could huddle and devise a strategy—one that she and the team executed quickly and professionally. As a leader, it gave me great comfort knowing that we had built a crisis communications structure that stood up to a real-time test.

Invest in your team when there are no urgent issues or crises. Make sure you carve out time and prioritize the drills we discussed earlier in this book. It works. Just as I needed quick support to help prevent an issue from becoming a crisis, you will too.

The Realities of Crisis Burnout

Burnout is a real problem with crisis communicators, especially in situations that keep your team in high gear and on high alert for long hours over consecutive days or weeks. If you see a team member showing signs of fatigue or lacking focus, consider that they could be on emotional overload, sleep-deprived, or suffering symptoms of stress.

I've supervised team members during a crisis who have found themselves struggling with what would otherwise have been fairly routine tasks, such as crafting a press release or completing a situation report. In those instances, I make a point of taking the person aside to find out what's actually going on. Maybe they've been working for fourteen hours straight without a break or have been too wound up to sleep even when they've managed to make it home. When someone hits their wall, the best thing you can do for them and the rest of the team is to temporarily relieve them of duty. Each of us needs time to rest so that we can come back ready to tackle the next task and the next.

If you do notice these signs and decide to send this person home to rest, be clear with them that your decision has nothing to do with a lack of confidence in their abilities. Rather, it's a decision you're making to relieve some of the pressure that is naturally emanating from the situation at hand. When you give team members permission to be human—that it's OK to acknowledge that they are suffering from burnout—you create a much healthier and ultimately more productive environment where people feel empowered to bring their best selves to work.

In fact, there's no better way to show that self-care and effective crisis management are compatible concepts than to set an example with your own behavior.

Cast Your Best Leadership Shadow

Making sure I modeled healthy behaviors for my team was something I had to be mindful of during the Indianapolis shooter crisis. After getting the late-night call and assembling the team, I spent the next few hours in a state of anxiously waiting for confirmation about casualties and injuries, the status of the shooter, and for the go-ahead from senior management to move forward with distributing statements and readying our next steps. Even though we were all running on adrenaline, the confusion and uncertainty surrounding the situation were exacting an emotional toll. There was no way that the team and I were going to be able to maintain this hyperalert state throughout the night and during what promised to be some difficult days ahead without respite. We were embarking on a marathon, and we had to pace ourselves if we were going to be effective.

> There's no better way to show that self-care and effective crisis management are compatible concepts than to set an example with your own behavior.

At around three in the morning, I decided that I needed to set an example and get a few hours of sleep. Leaving a designated leader in charge and with my cell phone on the nightstand next to my bed, with its ringtone on high volume, I went to sleep. By six in the morning, I was up getting my kids out the door for school, and by seven, I was back in the war room, ready to face whatever the day would bring.

Engaging in this type of self-care not only ensured that I would be better prepared to tackle what was certainly going to be a very long few days, but it also set the right example for my team. I had to show them that taking care of yourself is not only permissible; it's absolutely essential. Making sure that you're resting, that you're hydrated, and that you're taking in healthy nutrients to sustain your body and your mind is required if you're going to bring your best self to any situation. I needed my team to see that self-care is actually the opposite of slacking off on the job. It is the only way to maintain crucial competency during a crisis.

I spent time over the next few days asking them these questions on the side: Have you eaten today? When did you last sleep? How are you feeling? I also made sure everyone felt comfortable signing off for a few hours to take care of themselves and their families. Remember, we were still in the throes of the pandemic and working from home. As we all know, that came with additional challenges beyond the work that needed to be done.

As the crisis communications lead during the days that followed, I was also responsible for making sure the team knew they had my support, even before they would or could admit that they needed it. I remember that when I called one of our directors and asked that he go to the crime scene, I let him know that he was about to face what would probably be the hardest few days of his career and possibly his life. I told him that I was going to make myself available to him whenever he needed support, both during his execution of this difficult assignment and for a long time after his work was completed.

At the time, he wasn't exactly receptive to my offer of support. Like the rest of us, he was fixated on the problems at hand and running on adrenaline. As a team player who understood the gravity of what he was being asked to do, this director welcomed the opportunity to do his part and fulfill the mission as assigned, likely underestimating the emotional toll of the assignment. He said he appreciated the call and my offer of assistance but insisted that he was and would be fine. I reiterated that, no matter what, I was always available. I let him know that I was thankful for his willingness to fly to Indianapolis and fulfill this difficult assignment, and I assured him that my phone would be on and that I'd be available to him 24-7.

It wasn't easy to send him on this job knowing the somber challenges he was about to face, but someone had to be on the scene, and he could get there the fastest. As predicted, he ended up spending hours in a conference room with family members of the fallen victims, doing his best to offer support and assistance. By the time he called me the following day, it was apparent that he was both physically and emotionally drained. He freely admitted that, just as I had expected, this had been the hardest day of his life.

I listened as he recounted his day and offered up a heavy dose of gratitude and encouragement. I remember saying to him, "We're asking a lot of you. You're meeting with these families. You're going to be standing in front of the national media representing the company, showing the empathy and sympathy we all feel. Get through this. Keep that armor on, but when you get home, your job is to take care of yourself. That's going to be your top priority. Right now, it's about the company. Afterward, it has to be about you."

I made a point of staying in frequent contact with him for a while after his return home. I reminded him to take care of himself. I let him know that, even if he didn't want to talk about his experiences and feelings, he was not alone with them. He had someone who understood and supported him.

Fear of Missing Out

Those of us who are drawn to crisis communications tend to be the ones who seek out the adrenaline rush. We are the people you see running in the direction of the fire instead of away from it like everyone else. It's not that we welcome crises. Quite the contrary—we spend a lot of time and effort setting up systems to keep those fires from igniting in the first place. But once the flames erupt, we don't want to miss our chance to do our part in putting them out.

This natural propensity for wanting to participate in the solution translates into a heavy dose of FOMO. Because we spend so much time anticipating, planning for, and role-playing our rapid responses to disastrous events, we don't want to be left on the sidelines when the event we've drafted holding statements for and drilled on for hours actually comes to pass. We prepare so extensively that we feel ready for any emergent scenario that comes our way. We prepare until we no longer fear catastrophe. We know just what to do in a crisis situation. Now, instead of fearing a crisis, we fear missing out on the opportunity to do our part during a crisis. We feel obligated to be there; it is our duty and everything we trained for.

Not everyone who's prepared for a role in a crisis scenario is going to be physically present or available when the situation unfolds. A good communications leader needs to know how to manage the team members who aren't around to participate in managing a crisis, especially one that has a significant impact on the company or organization. That team member who was on extended leave when the tornado decimated your manufacturing facilities or the one who took their vacation just before the news broke that cybercriminals had hacked your customer database needs to still feel as though they are a valued member of the team upon their return.

Those of you who have managed through a crisis, especially if it was serious and lasted a long time, are going to have a bond around the crisis that those who weren't present won't share. It's your job to make sure those people who didn't have a chance to participate in managing the crisis don't feel excluded or guilty that they abandoned their team during a particularly trying time.

You might want to invite that team member to lead the postmortem of the event. The fact that they weren't able to participate in the actual crisis communications activities can lend a unique perspective as they lead the team's efforts in examining what occurred, what worked, and where improvements are warranted. The team member who missed out could also play a vital role in managing the event documentation repository and creating a checklist for similar crises in the future. The goal is to leverage the fact that they are able to look at the situation with a fresh perspective while also making them feel like a part of the significant event that transpired.

At the same time, you must be cognizant of having too many people working in a crisis. Sometimes, it needs to be a very small group because of the sensitivity of the situation. In that case, let the team members know they will be considered for future events, or ask them to run the normal business while you and other team members are pulled away to manage the situation. As we discussed in chapter seven, everyone wants to help and feel part of something bigger. Your job as the leader is to determine what you need in order to solve the immediate situation and take the rest as it comes.

Managing the Letdown

I spent half of my life performing in community theater before family and career became the priority for my time. It was fun and very hard work to get a show open. After spending long hours over many months with a group of people, there is a natural letdown and sense of sadness and loss when the show closes. I often feel those same feelings when a crisis is over and we all get back to business as usual.

Don't get me wrong, I accept and appreciate the rest and recovery time, but there is something special about being in a select group doing important work when the stakes are high. And this goes back to why crisis communicators run toward the fire, and once that fire is out, they look for the next one. During the time of the crisis, everyone is working together toward a clear goal. When you think about it, that is how we all want to work: in a high-functioning team doing important work and working at the speed of light to achieve the goal. So, you can see how there is a natural feeling of letdown once it is over.

As a leader, remember those feelings as you navigate the weeks following a crisis. The truth is that there is never enough time to thank your team properly for the work they did during a crisis.

So, what are some appropriate ways to thank a team for doing grueling and hard work around a situation they would just as soon forget? Here are some suggestions that I have used in the past:

- Take your team out to lunch or happy hour to show your appreciation. Sharing stories over a meal or drinks is a nice way to allow the team to feel like the work on a particular event is complete.

- Provide a monetary bonus or a gift card accompanied by a thank-you note.

- Consider a donation to the victims' fund. You can make this even more meaningful by donating a certain amount in each individual's name and honor.

- Make a gift of company-branded merchandise that team members would appreciate. Try to find something useful or that holds sentimental value.

Following the Indianapolis shooting crisis, we were looking for a way to thank the many people who had lent their support to help the company get through the crisis. It would have been great if we could have offered everyone a monetary bonus, but given that there were more than two hundred people we wanted to thank, that wasn't a viable option from a budgetary standpoint.

I started brainstorming with some of my team, and we came up with the idea to leverage FedEx's small business grant program to find a supplier or an independent artist to craft something special for those we wanted to thank. We reached out to the people who ran that program to see if they could recommend a small business that might be able to provide the kind of meaningful items that we could buy for thank-you gifts.

We were looking for some unique ideas, and we wanted to be thoughtful about the message we were sending. For instance, we didn't want to buy something commemorative, such as a keychain with the date of the tragedy. We didn't want that kind of stark reminder or something that would precipitate conversations about the tragedy. We wanted the focus to be on healing after the crisis and on how our community had come together to support each other. We wanted something that was uplifting.

Through the grant program, we were connected to a local Memphis artist whose signature was creating city skylines and producing them on handcrafted coffee mugs. We commissioned 250 handmade mugs showing the Indianapolis skyline and distributed them to each team member who had helped during the crisis. Along with the mug, each team member also received a personal letter from the CEO, thanking them for their work.

I cherish my Indianapolis skyline mug to this day, and I hope that the others who received one do as well. It is a reminder of the team members we lost and the important work that was done to help the community heal.

There are many creative ways to thank your team for doing great work and to help them feel valued. Choose one that works for your organization and is appropriate for the circumstances, and run with it. Your team will appreciate it more than you realize.

CHAPTER NINE

Postcrisis Management: Lessons Learned

Crisis communications management is a never-ending exercise in continuous improvement. No matter how much you plan for a crisis, how often you conduct drills of different scenarios, and how well you execute your crisis communications plan, there are going to be things that work and things that don't. Situations unfold in unpredictable ways, and best-laid plans aside, there are going to be new lessons to learn from each crisis you encounter.

Those lessons—especially if you've made the effort to document your progress during the crisis and then conduct a meaningful postmortem review—will act as change agents to inform your team's progress and enhance its abilities. If practice makes permanent, then a thorough and honest postcrisis review embeds that permanence into your team's DNA. It becomes muscle memory.

Postcrisis reviews are also important to preserve institutional memory in the event your company faces legal action. Memories can be unreliable, and perceptions can become skewed with the passage of time. Detailed documentation during the crisis, followed by careful review, is the best way to ensure the preservation of facts. I often revisit postcrisis documentation when preparing for a potential issue. I shared an example earlier in the book about using previous learnings to prepare for weather-related events at the university.

> If practice makes permanent, then a thorough and honest postcrisis review embeds that permanence into your team's DNA.

Without that detailed information, I would have been far less prepared, and the university would have had to rely on what team members remembered doing versus having access to thorough documentation on what transpired and, more importantly, the lessons learned.

Documentation is also the perfect resource for establishing a tabletop drill or a scenario-planning exercise. Look at what happened, think through what could have gone wrong but didn't, and test out that situation with your team. Remember at the end of the last chapter when I talked about the disappointed team members who missed out on participating in the crisis? Chances are high that you will reference that crisis again, use it as a teaching opportunity, and share it with new team members. Having documentation is the fastest way to get everyone on the same page when you want or need to reference the event. Even those who were part of the crisis will benefit from the documents to help refresh their memories of important details.

Finally, your postcrisis management and documentation reviews are not just for the benefit of the crisis management team. They can help your entire organization better navigate a crisis situation.

Toward that end, you will want to share what you've learned with all the impacted areas and departments throughout your company. What areas were affected by the crisis, and how did the actions of the crisis management and communications teams help or hinder each department before, during, and after the crisis?

When conducting your review, step into the shoes of different company teams to assess the impact of how the crisis unfolded and was managed from their perspectives. Were operations suspended or shut down? What did this do to productivity, customer support, and sales? Did human resources get what it needed to fulfill its obligations to the company's management and employees during the crisis? Keep these internal stakeholders top of mind while you're doing your postcrisis review work.

Conduct Your Internal Review Sooner Rather Than Later

The further away you get from a crisis, the more likely the details of what occurred will fade. The more time that transpires between a crisis situation and taking an honest and detailed look at what worked and what didn't, the more likely you are to forget the important lessons learned from the experience. If you don't review what occurred and reflect on the significance of what transpired shortly following the relevant events, you risk losing the opportunity to turn those lessons into institutional knowledge.

Striking while the proverbial iron is hot is why I recommend conducting your postmortems as thoroughly as possible and as quickly as possible after the acute phase of the crisis ends. The danger of waiting until everything is back to normal—a state that could take days, weeks, months, or even years to achieve—is that memories will fade and people, in the retelling, will overlook small but important details. It's human nature to remember the good and bury the bad. If you wait too long, the retelling of events will gloss over important details, and that won't help build the knowledge base your company needs to keep improving. You are looking for facts, not folklore.

Every member of the team needs to contribute to the postcrisis review process. This includes your internal and external communications teams and any outside consultants you brought in to assist with managing the crisis, as well as those involved in the crisis management efforts from legal, operations, human resources, and any other functional areas of your company. If they were involved in any way in getting the company through the crisis, they need a seat at the table.

It's important to make sure your legal representative is present. The role of legal counsel at the postmortem is to offer guidance on the preservation of information in the event it ends up having an evidentiary value in a lawsuit or other legal matter. Your legal team needs to determine what records must be preserved and what information should be safeguarded as privileged, business confidential, or protected intellectual property.

Best Time to Hold Your Review

The time to start looking at how events unfolded and how the crisis management team responded is when you've reached the place where the matter is contained and you're no longer scrambling to keep up with media requests, address immediate stakeholder needs, and respond to other urgent matters. The time to start looking in the rearview mirror is when you find yourself starting to recalibrate your focus on what lies ahead.

In the case of the FedEx Indianapolis shooter, we started doing our postcrisis work about two weeks after the event. By that time, the acute crisis had subsided, although we were still dealing with the aftermath of the incident—assisting with memorial services, promoting the victims' fund, and working with internal and external stakeholders to make sure that impacted families and FedEx employees were being cared for. But for the most part, the round-the-clock frenzy had subsided, and we had gotten back to our normal work routines. When people had returned to a normal work cadence, I knew that the acute phase was over, and it was time to convene a postcrisis meeting.

How you should go about managing a postcrisis internal review is going to depend on the nature of the crisis you're reviewing and how many people are going to be included in the meeting.

Setting Clear Parameters

Managing the postmortem of how your company handled a cybersecurity breach or a notification of a federal grant cancellation is going to be different from convening a postcrisis meeting in the aftermath of catastrophic flooding or a violent crime at your place of business. The greater the physical and emotional toll a crisis takes on your team—that is, the more they take what occurred personally—the greater the potential for an emotionally charged review session.

As discussed in chapter eight, a responsible leader strives to be mindful of the emotional and physical distress that accompanies the management of a crisis, especially one that has heart-wrenching consequences. There is a time and a place for emotionally supporting your team and helping them find the tools they need to process difficult experiences. But the postcrisis meeting is not one of these times. Take your team out to lunch or dinner and let them share their war stories about the event. It is important for some people to process their emotions verbally, so give them a safe place to do that outside of a postcrisis meeting.

Postcrisis review sessions are critical to the growth and success of your crisis communications team. These reviews help you and your team members learn from the most recent crisis so you can increase your effectiveness when the next one happens. If you don't want your postcrisis review to turn into an impromptu group therapy session, you're going to have to set clear meeting parameters from the outset. This includes determining the setting for your meeting and who will be participating and preparing an agenda in advance.

Organizing Your Postcrisis Meeting

There are several ways you can go about conducting a postcrisis meeting. One way is to gather everyone in one space to present their specific perspectives on what transpired. You can get away with this kind of informal sharing session if your group is relatively small. My rule of thumb is if the group consists of twelve people or fewer, I allow a bit of leeway for give-and-take during the meeting. If the group is larger, I establish a clear agenda with an accompanying timetable.

Even if you're inviting a small group to a brainstorming session, it's good to establish some rules of engagement. Make sure everyone is clear that this is not the time or place to vent frustrations, air grievances, or discuss emotionally charged issues. Instead, the postcrisis review is a time to discuss roles, processes, and delivery systems.

For this kind of brainstorming session, it's good practice to appoint a scribe—you can use a person, AI, or a combination of the two—to capture what everyone is saying. Even though the meeting is on the informal side, you're still going to want a record of what transpired so you can determine what worked, what didn't, and what improvements can be made in the future.

If you're convening a larger group, I recommend setting a formal agenda for a postcrisis review meeting. When I convene postcrisis meetings with a large number of participants, I ask the leads of each area (the ones I had assigned at the onset of the crisis event) to present the highlights of the lessons learned broken down into different time frames. If your event is of the size and scope of what we experienced with the Indianapolis shooting, you may decide to convene several sessions, all following a similar format. Here is how I handled the postcrisis meetings after the Indianapolis incident.

First, I opened each meeting by acknowledging the incident and its effect on not only the company but also each member of the team. I also acknowledged that reliving some of what transpired might be difficult. I let the attendees know that while we needed to keep the meeting professional and on task, anyone feeling overwhelmed who needed to take a break could do so.

Second, I asked each lead to relay their perceptions of how well the team pivoted into crisis mode. Some of us were called into action in the middle of the night. Others found out about what had occurred at the start of their workday. How prepared was the team to switch into crisis mode and address the situation? As team members tapped out to get rest while others took their place, how well did the passing of the baton work? Were there any gaps that we could avoid in the future?

Next, we broke down the timeline of events and discussed what transpired during the first twenty-four hours after the shooting and then how matters were handled over the next few days. We talked about the development of initial holding statements, the challenges of staying informed as details began to emerge, and any difficulties encountered in providing timely and accurate information to senior management. As we went through the agenda, each person had the opportunity to talk about what worked, what didn't, and what could have been done to improve the situation.

Throughout these meetings, people were extremely honest, self-aware, and forthcoming. It's been my experience that if you create a safe and professional environment, your team members will welcome opportunities to contribute their best insights and observations to the postcrisis process.

Gathering Insights from Outside Stakeholders

As communications professionals, our first instincts are always to put as much distance as possible between our company and anything that reflects negatively on our brand. Since one of our primary missions is to preserve our brand and reputation in the face of adversity, seeking postcrisis review insights from outside stakeholders—such as shareholders, customers, vendors, industry groups, and investors—seems counterintuitive. The last thing we want to do is prolong perceptions of a negative situation. No postcrisis review, however, is going to be complete without the input of these stakeholders.

The best way to approach stakeholders is through the individuals within your organization who know them best. For example, you'll want a representative from your investor relations department to reach out to a select group of shareholders for feedback. Ask your CEO to conduct a postmortem with board members and encourage your salespeople to reach out to the customers with whom they have solid relationships to gauge reactions and sentiments. Arm these representatives with a list of questions that will help you determine these stakeholders' perceptions of your company before, during, and then after the crisis.

You will also want to review the activity on your social media platforms, leveraging any social media monitoring tools you might use, such as Sprout Social, Hootsuite, or Buffer, if available. For smaller companies, many of these social monitoring platforms are free to begin using, so it is worth checking out. If you don't have anything in place before a crisis event, you can conduct an audit of activity before, during, and after the incident to get a feel for the public's perception of your company's performance in managing the crisis and how it might have affected your brand.

Analyzing Inputs and Implementing Improvements

The purpose of compiling feedback is to help you make informed decisions regarding the efficacy of various elements of your crisis plan. Rarely, if ever, will the feedback suggest that you should discard your existing plan and start fresh. Rather, you're going to be able to isolate instances where you can enhance elements of your plan and incorporate the lessons learned to inform future crises. The goal is to enhance and refine your plan as needed.

If, for example, you hear loud and clear during your internal crisis review that you could have done a better job with internal communications, then you'll want to do a follow-up to capture more details so you can incorporate those lessons learned into a revised plan. As another example, after completing our crisis review following the Indianapolis incident, we were able to identify individuals who we could have turned to for help in facilitating quicker decision-making. We also identified areas where we would have been better served by slowing down and waiting for additional input before moving forward. We took that feedback and made adjustments to our plan.

The action items emanating from a postmortem review can be subtle but poignant. Sometimes, moving the needle just a bit can make all the difference. Of course, not everything you learn during the internal review will require further inquiry or a revision to your plan. Not every observation is going to translate into a process improvement. But you still want to capture and analyze as much as you can. It's always better to have more information than you need than not enough information to effect change where necessary.

You can also incorporate what you have learned into your next crisis simulation. If you think things could have gone a different way with a change to your protocols, practice with those changes incorporated into your simulation and keep raising the stakes to see just how far you can go.

The information you receive from external sources can be extremely valuable in gauging and responding to any threats to your reputation. If the feedback indicates that the public has lost trust in your company or your brand, you'll want to explore recovery mechanisms for repairing or rebuilding.

Let's say you've had a data breach that wasn't your fault. Even though you can prove that the breach was unavoidable, that doesn't change the fact that your customers are upset and concerned about the repercussions of the breach.

This is the case even when you've followed the crisis plan by immediately informing them of the breach and putting new measures in place to shore up your systems so it won't happen again. Based on your postcrisis review, you determine that you need to focus on rebuilding trust, so you decide to provide customers whose data was compromised with a free credit monitoring service and offer them additional incentives to stay with your company. Without the postcrisis stakeholder input, you might not have realized that these additional steps were necessary to rebuild consumer confidence until it was too late and you lost customers.

Postcrisis Review for Crisis Avoidance

Often, the information you document during a crisis and then collect during a postcrisis review will serve to mitigate the effects of similar circumstances in the future. This intelligence could even help your organization prevent a crisis from occurring.

The University of Memphis did such a great job documenting the 2024 severe winter weather event that when we got word that a major weather event was predicted, we were able to use our improved winter weather crisis management plan to address every conceivable contingency to protect our students, faculty, staff, and campus infrastructure. While the subsequent event didn't reach crisis levels, we felt secure that we had the situation fully under control and kept everyone properly informed.

Using Postcrisis Reviews to Pay It Forward

Very few people willingly walk into a crisis situation. But if you find yourself embroiled in one, you might as well make it count. As I've said before, you should never waste a good crisis.

Each time I find myself conducting a crisis management postmortem, examining what went right and what could have gone better, I gather more insights, garner more wisdom, and walk away with a greater understanding of how to be an even more effective crisis communicator. So, whenever possible, I embrace opportunities to share what I've learned with others.

After Indianapolis, I was invited to participate in a fireside chat with an organization of similarly situated communications professionals I'd been involved with for years as a member. I shared my experiences and answered their questions. They wanted to know what my team and I had gone through to prepare for a possible active shooter scenario, how we managed the actual crisis—including how and if our drills were actually beneficial in preparing us for the real thing—and how we faced certain challenges with managing both internal and external communications during a highly volatile and fluid situation.

Following my time at FedEx, I started my own consulting firm. In developing the content for my website, I had to think through and articulate the value of the services I have to offer. When it comes to crisis communications management, the best way to get through a crisis is to have been through one. Short of that, look for someone who has been through a crisis and ask for help. That was when the idea of this book was born. Sharing what I have learned in order to help others is important to me.

Throughout my career, I've been called upon to share the knowledge and experiences I've gleaned from working through various crises. In my experience, each time I've shared my knowledge of crisis communication management—whether it was through having a fireside chat, participating in a panel presentation, penning a thought leadership article, or even writing this book—I've ended up receiving much more than I've given.

If the first rule of crisis communications is "do no harm," then the last rule is "leave things better than you found them." You can't always fix the crisis in front of you, but if you can take what you've learned and share that with others, then you've done just that: You've made it better for the next person. As you progress as a crisis communications lead, I encourage you to look for ways to share your own wisdom and insights with people, both inside and outside of your organization.

CHAPTER
TEN

Creating Your Crisis Management Tool Kit

When it comes to preparing your company and your team to manage communications through a crisis, I can't overemphasize how important it is to have a plan in place and commit to actively and consistently working on and revising that plan. A crisis communications management plan is a living, breathing document. It requires constant attention. As your business grows and changes, so should your crisis management plan.

Revise Your Plan Often

Each time you confront a new issue or work through a unique situation, you're going to have new information and insights that can be used to enhance your plan. Take your situation and postcrisis reports and use the information to update your plan.

Complacency is the enemy of crisis communications. Even if you haven't had an occasion to activate your plan yet, at the very least, I recommend that you take a comprehensive look at it on a quarterly basis. Chances are that some of the information contained in the plan will have become obsolete or irrelevant. For example, if there's been a change in senior management, you might need to revise your internal communications flow. If your own team has grown or you've had to replace a team member, you'll need to revise relevant sections pertaining to job functions within your department. Maybe your company has introduced a new product line that requires a new type or level of regulatory compliance, increasing risk exposure. Most companies are constantly changing, so your crisis plan should be constantly changing as well.

> Complacency is the enemy of crisis communications.

Keep Up with Your Tabletop Drills

Keeping your plan updated and current is only half of the equation, though. If you're truly going to create a meaningful crisis management protocol for your company, you need to test your plan under different scenarios. This is why it's so important to continue with your tabletop drills. This takes discipline and requires proactive planning, but it is worth it. It doesn't matter how you conduct your drills—they can be as simple or as complex as you have the time, budget, and interest for—but commit to doing them on a regular basis.

I once participated in a workplace shooting simulation that was incredibly thorough, so much so that the organizers included a video of actual employees pretending to talk to the media to introduce new complexities to the simulation. These types of professional-produced sessions are impactful but also take months of preparation, require staff to support their development, and can require a significant budget to execute. You don't have to go over the top to produce a successful drill.

Some of the most beneficial tabletop simulations I've engaged in have involved my small crisis team sitting around a table and challenging each other to come up with situations that were probable as we competed with each other to see who could add the most far-fetched twists to test our skills. We would dedicate staff meetings each month to test the next person's scenario. Conducting drills on a regular schedule doesn't have to be complicated. But it is necessary. The point is to find a way to do these exercises on a consistent basis and then take what you learn from them and revise your crisis plan accordingly.

Start Building Your Crisis Communications Plan

As the saying goes, the journey of a thousand miles starts with a single step. I'm providing you with a crisis communications plan outline as a first step in creating your own personalized plan. The outline below is far from comprehensive, but it hits all the major points discussed throughout this book and should serve you well as an initial launchpad for developing your own plan.

Before you begin, though, think about the objectives you want to set for your organization. Why does your organization need a crisis plan? Some obvious ones that come to mind include protecting your employees, securing your physical assets, and preventing damage to your company's good reputation. These are quite general, of course. Try to state your objectives in detail, taking into account your specific industry, geographic location, and core values and competencies. Knowing the "why" of a crisis management plan helps inform what you want to protect and how to go about protecting what you've identified as valuable.

If you already have an established plan, my challenge for you is to conduct an audit of your current crisis management resources, compare it to the outline below, and identify gaps. Then, schedule a crisis simulation exercise, focusing on a previously untested aspect of your updated plan.

CRISIS COMMUNICATIONS PLAN OUTLINE

1. Identify Potential Crisis Scenarios

Start by listing possible crises your organization might face, such as

- **operational crises:** product recalls, cyberattacks, equipment malfunctions, and service outages;
- **reputational crises:** executive scandals, employee misconduct, negative media coverage, and viral social posts;
- **legal and regulatory crises:** lawsuits and compliance violations;
- **workforce issues:** strikes, layoffs, discrimination claims, and workplace accidents; and
- **environmental and health crises:** natural disasters, pandemics, and workplace accidents.

2. Establish a Crisis Response Team

Define key roles and responsibilities, including the following:

- **Spokesperson(s):** Who will serve as the face of the organization and speak to the media?
- **Legal counsel:** Who will ensure compliance with regulations and provide advice to mitigate lawsuits?
- **PR and communications team:** Who will craft messages, field questions, and manage media relations?
- **Social media team:** Who will monitor online conversations, measure sentiment, and respond appropriately?
- **Crisis communications lead:** Who is the point person to lead the communications team? This does not have to be the leader of the organization, but the role should be designated so that everyone understands where decisions are being made.

- **Scribe:** Who on the team will serve as the notetaker and prepare your situation reports, collect media statements, and capture details during the postcrisis meeting? Keep in mind that this role can be shared so that a single person isn't responsible for all.

- **Functional lead:** This person sits on the crisis management team to act as the bridge between the operations team and the communications team. They attend all meetings and bring updates to the crisis communications lead.

- **External support:** Who are the consultants or experts you may need during a crisis event? Establish the process to engage these experts if and when you need them.

- **Activation plan:** Will you use Zoom, Microsoft Teams, or another online platform to serve as your virtual war room? Have you identified everyone who should be activated to join the war room? Do you have a current contact list?

Note: Training your team is an important process. Team preparedness should include training and tabletop exercises to ensure everyone knows what to do and how to activate the crisis plan if needed. See chapter three, Practice Makes Permanence, for more information.

3. Develop Preapproved Messaging

Prepare **holding statements** that can be quickly adapted for different scenarios. See chapter three for more on preparing a statement database.

General holding statement:

We are aware of the situation and are actively investigating. Our top priority is the safety and well-being of our team, and we will share updates as they become available.

4. Establish a Media Management Protocol

Define **who speaks**, **when**, **and how**. Key elements include the following:

- **Media policy:** Only authorized spokespeople should speak to the press.
- **Press statement templates:** Have adaptable press release templates.
- **Press conference guidelines:** Determine when and how to hold a media briefing.
- **Interview prep:** Prepare spokespeople with key talking points and Q&A documents. Conduct media training in advance.
- **Media monitoring:** Establish media monitoring protocols and provide media briefings in daily reports.

5. Establish an Internal Communication Plan

- Inform employees before the media.
- Ensure consistency in messaging.
- Provide a **crisis FAQ** for internal use.

We understand you may have questions. We are committed to transparency and will update you regularly. If you receive media inquiries, please refer them to [PR contact].

6. Implement a Social Media Strategy

- Monitor sentiment in real time.
- Have **predrafted responses** for social media use. This can often be your holding statement or media statement.
- Address misinformation swiftly.
- Provide social media analytics in the situation reports at the end of each day.

7. **Plan for Postcrisis Recovery**
   - Assess the effectiveness of your response.
   - Conduct a **postcrisis review**: What worked? What needs improvement?
   - Rebuild trust through **transparency and corrective actions**.

8. **Store in an Accessible Format**

Your tool kit should be

   - digital (shared drive or crisis app),
   - printed (for emergency access), and
   - regularly updated to include the latest information for anyone following.

Final Words

Anyone new to crisis communications is bound to feel intimidated at times. While dealing with emergencies and high-stakes situations can be exhilarating, it can also feel overwhelming and exhausting. When I said before that my initial four months in a crisis communications role felt like five years, I meant it.

I want you to know that you can do this. Think about what you've already been through in your life and how you've gotten through every challenge you've faced so far.

We all had a crash course in crisis management during COVID-19. I doubt very many of you like spending time thinking about all that you went through during the pandemic, but it was full of valuable lessons and learning. We all learned to be adaptable and resilient. Through those weeks, months, and years, we all learned to decipher what was true and what wasn't. We had to sift through the clutter of information and misinformation to find what worked for us, our families, and our companies. That is what managing a crisis is all about.

When information is coming at you at one hundred miles per hour, having the ability to take it in, sort through it all to find the important things, and develop an action plan is exactly what you need during a crisis event. So, when you are in the moment of a crisis, take a deep breath and remember that you have been here before. And while perhaps it is not the exact same circumstance, deep down, you know that you can get through what you are facing. COVID-19 is your proof.

Think of the tools that I've provided in this book as your guide to organizing and executing a crisis communications strategy. That's all you really need. You've already developed enough resilience and muscle memory to see your company through any crisis that comes your way.

ABOUT THE AUTHOR

Michele Ehrhart is a seasoned communications and marketing executive with more than three decades of experience driving strategic reputation management for organizations across various sectors. Currently serving as the senior vice president and chief marketing and communications officer at the University of Memphis, Michele leads the development and execution of the university's branding, marketing, and communications strategy. She has a proven track record of overseeing award-winning communications campaigns, including global media relations, executive communications, social media, and crisis management for a Fortune 50 company.

Throughout her career, Michele has been a catalyst for change, championing talent, transforming organizational culture, and leading teams of more than seventy professionals. Her passion lies in creating and executing innovative marketing strategies that align business objectives and organizational values. With a deep commitment to excellence and leadership, she continues to drive impactful results and inspire positive transformation in every organization she has worked with.

Michele lives in Memphis, Tennessee, with her husband, two children, and a labradoodle named Lark.